The Reader's Digest
Children's
WORLD
ATLAS

Previous page: Mont St Michel in Normandy, France
Opposite page: Planting rice in Thailand

Cover:
Masai woman, Kenya/Tony Stone Worldwide

A Reader's Digest Book designed and edited by
Ilex Publishers Limited

Based on *The Children's World Atlas,* published by
Reader's Digest (Australia) Pty. Ltd. (Inc. in N.S.W.)

Copyright © 1991 Ilex Publishers Limited

Revised and reprinted 1992

Library of Congress Cataloging in Publication Data

The Reader's digest children's world atlas/[text by Malcolm Day,
Kate Woodward and Philip Steele: Illustrated by Janos Marffy and
Chris Rothero: maps produced by Euromap Limited].
    p.   cm.
    "Based on The children's world atlas, published by Reader's Digest
Press (Australia) — Half title
    "Designed and edited by Ilex Publishers Limited — Half title
    Includes index.
    Summary: An introduction to regional geography of the world, with
a map, facts, and pictures for the major regions of each continent.
    ISBN 0-89577-388-0
    1. Atlases. [1. Atlases.] I. Day, Malcolm. II. Woodward,
Kate. III. Steele, Philip. 1948–. IV. Marffy, Janos, 1930–
ill. V. Rothero, Christopher, ill. VI. Euromap Limited.
VII. Reader's digest. VIII. Title: Children's world atlas.
G1021.R57 1991
912—dc20   90-28667

Text by Malcolm Day, Kate Woodward, and Philip Steele
Designed by Richard Rowan
Edited by Nicola Barber and Nicholas Harris
Maps produced by Euromap Limited and Alan Mais
Illustrated by Janos Marffy (Jillian Burgess Artists) and
Chris Rothero (Linden Artists)

The heading strips in this book illustrate a representative scene from each region;
Page 26 Toronto, Ontario, Canada; p28 Lake Ontario, Canada; p30 Rocky Mountains, Canada;
p32 New York, N.Y., U.S.; p36 Boston, Massachusetts, U.S.; p38 Mount Rushmore, South
Dakota, U.S.; p40 Texas oilfields, U.S.; p42 Canyon lands U.S.; p44 Chichén Itzá, Mexico;
p46 Caribbean beach; p50 Machu Picchu, Peru; p52 Rio de Janeiro, Brazil; p54 Atacama
Desert, Chile; p60 Iceland; p62 Carew Castle, Wales; p64 Eiffel Tower, Paris; p66 Windmills,
the Netherlands; p68 River Rhine, Germany; p70 Matterhorn, Switzerland; p72 Leaning
Tower, Pisa, Italy; p74 Sagrada Familia, Barcelona, Spain; p76 Acropolis, Athens, Greece;
p78 Budapest, Hungary; p80 St. Basil's Cathedral, Moscow, Russia; p88 Blue Mosque,
Istanbul, Turkey; p90 Oasis, Saudi Arabia; p92 Village scene, Iran; p94 Taj Mahal, India;
p96 Terraced fields, Indonesia; p98 Guilin, China; p102 Mount Fuji, Japan; p106 The Sphinx
and a Pyramid, Egypt; p108 Kilimanjaro, Tanzania; p110 Cape Town, South Africa; p114 The
harbor, Sydney, Australia; p116 Rotorua, New Zealand; p118 Easter Island, Pacific; p120
Antarctica.

Printed in Spain

The Reader's Digest
Children's
WORLD
ATLAS

The Reader's Digest Association, Inc.
Pleasantville, New York/Montreal

CONTENTS

HOW TO USE THIS ATLAS

In this atlas the world is divided up into six parts: the continents of North America, South America, Europe, Asia, and Africa, and the region known as Oceania which includes Australasia and the islands of the Pacific. At the beginning of each section you will find a political map showing the countries which make up each continent or region, together with facts and figures telling you about the area, population, and capital of each of these countries. On the following pages, physical maps illustrate the land's surface, showing mountains, forests, deserts, ice, savanna, steppe, and cultivated land.

To find out what the colors, symbols, and abbreviations on the maps in this book mean, check the key on this page. If you want to look up a place, either on a map or in the text of this atlas, use the indexes at the back of the book.

Look at the location map to find out the position of a country or region in the world.

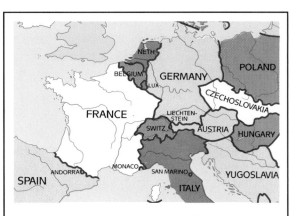

A political map shows how the world is divided into different countries.

KEY
Physical environments

Forest

Savanna/steppe/ cultivated land

Desert

Mountains

Tundra

Ice

Country border

State boundary

Ottawa ■
Capital city

Milan ●
City (population over 1 million)

Puebla ●
City (population under 1 million)

Salem □
State capital

Olympus ▲ 9551
Mountain and height in feet

Brenner Pass
Mountain pass

River

Seasonal river

Lake

Seasonal lake

Canal

Scale

0   300 Km

0   200 Miles

Map abbreviations
Arch.	Archipelago
Aust.	Australia
Br.	(Great) Britain
C.	Cape
Fr.	France
I.	Island
Is.	Islands
L.	Lake
Mt.	Mount
Mts.	Mountains
Neth.	Netherlands
N.Z.	New Zealand
Pen.	Peninsula
Pk.	Peak
Port.	Portugal
Pt.	Point
Sp.	Spain

A physical map shows the mountains, lakes, deserts, forests, and grasslands that cover the Earth's surface.

Text abbreviations
mi.	miles
sq. mi.	square miles
ft.	feet
in.	inches
km.	kilometers
sq. km.	square kilometers
m.	meters
cm.	centimeters

To work out real distances between two places measure the distance on the map and then compare it to the bar scale.

Height of land
Maps on pages 28-31 and 36-43

feet		meters
13,000		4000
10,000		3050
6500		2000
3000		900
1500		450
500		150
Below sea level 0		0

5

PLANET EARTH

Large groups of stars, gas, and dust are called galaxies, and there maybe over 100 billion galaxies in the Universe. Our local galaxy is called the Milky Way, and it contains billions of stars. The Sun is just one of these stars, a tiny speck in the vastness of space.

However, if the Sun is compared with the planet Earth, it seems huge. The nine known planets of the Solar System orbit around this great ball of burning gas, which provides the warmth that makes life possible on Earth. Many of the planets are themselves orbited by moons. Earth has only one moon, but it has been proved that Uranus has at least 15, Jupiter 17 and Saturn at least 18. Other objects within the Solar System include the asteroids, over 3000 tiny planets and rock fragments which orbit mainly between Mars and Jupiter.

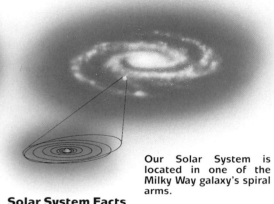

Our Solar System is located in one of the Milky Way galaxy's spiral arms.

Solar System Facts

Planet	Diameter (mi. (kms.))	Time taken to orbit the Sun
Mercury	3100 (4878)	88 days
Venus	7521 (12,104)	224.7 days
Earth	7916 (12,740)	365.4 days
Mars	4212 (6739)	687 days
Jupiter	88,000 (141,622)	11.9 years
Saturn	71,000 (114,263)	29.5 years
Uranus	32,116 (51,800)	84 years
Neptune	30,642 (49,424)	164.8 years
Pluto	1500 (2414)	247.7 years

The inner planets

In 1976, two American Viking spacecraft landed on Mars, 60 million miles distant from Earth. They revealed a barren, rocky landscape, with air reddened by suspended dust but found no evidence that life ever existed there. Earth is the only planet in the Solar System where life is possible. The surface of Venus, Earth's nearest neighbor, is baking hot. Its poisonous clouds float in a dense atmosphere. Mercury, nearest planet to the Sun, has a very thin atmosphere.

The Solar System

Pluto
Neptune
Uranus
Comet
Meteroids
Asteroids
Saturn
Mars
Jupiter
Venus
Sun
Earth
Mercury

The Earth: our home planet

The center of the Earth is called the core. The inner part of the core is thought to be made up of a great ball consisting mostly of solid iron, extending about 3950 miles from the center. The metals of the core are intensely hot, with a temperature of about 10,800 degrees Fahrenheit. In the outer part of the core, a layer about 3200 miles thick, the metals are liquid. The whole core is surrounded by the mantle, a great layer of rock about 1800 miles thick. The surface of the Earth is called the crust and is a thin layer of rock. Some ocean floors rest on crust only 4 miles thick, but at its thickest, beneath the great masses of land, the crust is 43 miles deep.

The outer shell of the Earth is made up of sections called plates. The great heat from the Earth's center makes these plates move. Normally, this happens so slowly that we do not notice it. Over millions of years the edges of some of these plates squeeze against each other, pushing up ranges of mountains. Sometimes, if a sudden movement occurs at the boundaries of the plates an earthquake takes place. Then, the earth shakes and cracks open beneath our feet.

Above the land and sea, the atmosphere extends 300 miles into space. This layer of air is a mixture of gases which includes nitrogen, oxygen, argon, carbon dioxide, and water vapor. Air, soil and water are warmed and lit by the rays of the Sun, 93 million miles away in space. The atmosphere screens out many other rays which might harm life on Earth.

The Earth rotates on its axis every day. The part facing the Sun is in daylight, while the other side of the Earth has night. The planet takes 365 days and six hours to orbit the Sun.

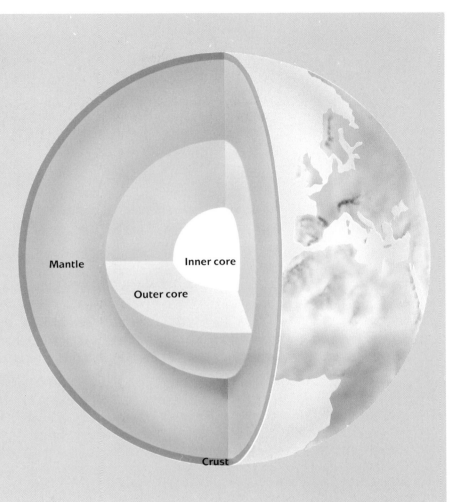

Mantle

Inner core

Outer core

Crust

The outer planets

Some astronomers think that there may be ten planets, but only nine have been discovered so far. Each planet spins around as it orbits the Sun. Tiny Pluto, smaller than our Moon, is normally the farthest from the Sun. However, at times its orbit swings in nearer to the Sun than that of Neptune. Uranus is tilted over on its side. Saturn is famous for its beautiful rings, made up of dust and ice; they were first identified by the Dutch astronomer, Christiaan Huygens, in 1655. Jupiter is the largest planet in the Solar System. It is a planet of violent storms, one of which forms a great swirling red spot that can be seen through a telescope from Earth. Both Saturn and Jupiter are covered by oceans of liquid hydrogen.

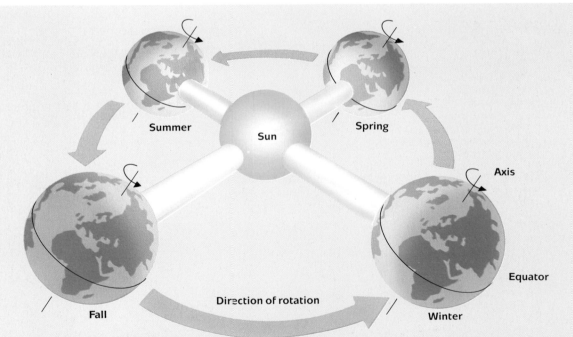

Summer

Sun

Spring

Axis

Equator

Fall

Direction of rotation

Winter

The four seasons

The imaginary line around which a planet spins is called the axis. The Earth's axis is tilted from the upright by an angle of 23°27'. This means that as the Earth travels through space, parts of its surface are tilted towards the Sun. These regions enjoy a summer season, with warm weather and long hours of daylight. Later in the year, they begin to tilt away from the Sun and the season turns to fall. During the short, cold days of winter these regions are farther from the Sun. The spring season brings back warmth and light as they begin to tile towards the Sun once again. In the tropical regions, which lie along the Equator, there is less seasonal contrast.

THE PHYSICAL WORLD

This physical map of the world illustrates the surface of the Earth with its mountains, plains, deserts, lakes, and rivers. Over two thirds of the Earth's surface is covered by water. There are four vast oceans, the Pacific, Atlantic, Indian, and Arctic. The seas surrounding Antarctica are sometimes counted as a fifth, known as the Southern Ocean. On this map the biggest ocean, the Pacific, is split into two.

Features in *relief* stand out on the map. You will see the Himalaya mountain range which contains the highest peaks in the world, and major river systems such as the Nile in Africa and the Amazon in South America. The gold-colored areas represent the dry expanses of deserts, such as the Sahara, the Gobi in central Asia, the arid lands of the Australian interior, and the driest place on Earth, the Atacama Desert in Chile.

Regions of the World	Area		Approximate Population
	sq.mi.	(sq.km.)	
North America (including Mexico and Central America)	9,785,000	(25,349,000)	500,000,000
South America	6,798,000	(17,611,000)	300,000,000
Europe (including European Russia)	4,053,300	(10,498,000)	500,000,000
Asia (including Asian Russia)	17,400,000	(45,066,000)	3,000,000,000
Africa	11,709,000	(30,335,000)	600,000,000
Oceania	3,444,278	(8,923,000)	25,000,000
Antarctica	5,149,240	(13,340,000)	

Earth Facts
Distance around the Equator 24,902mi. (40,074km.)
Distance around the Poles 24,860mi. (40,008km.)
Distance to the center of the Earth 3958mi. (6370km.)
Average distance from the Earth to the Sun 93,210,000mi. (150,000,000km.)
Average distance from the Earth to the Moon 238,857mi. (384,403km.)
Speed at which the Earth orbits the Sun 18.5mi. per second (29.8km. per second)
Total surface area of the Earth 196,836,000sq.mi. (509,803,110sq.km.)
Total land area of the Earth 55,786,000sq.mi. (144,485,136sq.km.)
Total area of water on the Earth 141,050,000sq.mi. (365,318,000sq.km.)
Coldest recorded temperature on the Earth Vostok, Antarctica (−128.6°F/−89.2°C)
Hottest recorded temperature on the Earth San Luis, Mexico (136°F/57.8°C)
Place on the Earth with the highest average rainfall Mount Waialeale, Hawaii (average annual rainfall 460in./1168cm.)
Driest place on the Earth Atacama Desert, Chile (no rain from 1570–1971)

Largest Lakes

	Area	
	sq.mi.	(sq.km.)
Caspian Sea (Asia)	143,630	(372,000)
Superior (Canada/U.S.A.)	31,795	(82,348)
Victoria (Africa)	26,828	(69,484)
Aral (Asia)	25,500	(66,044)
Huron (Canada/U.S.A.)	23,430	(60,700)
Michigan (U.S.A)	22,395	(58,020)
Tanganyika (Africa)	13,860	(32,900)

Largest Deserts

	Area	
	sq.mi.	(sq.km.)
Sahara (northern Africa)	3,475,000	(9,000,000)
Australian	600,000	(1,554,000)
Arabian	500,000	(1,295,000)
Gobi (central Asia)	500,000	(1,295,000)
Kalahari (southern Africa)	225,000	(583,000)

Highest Waterfalls

	Drop	
	ft.	(m.)
Angel Falls (Venezuela)	3212	(979)
Tugela Falls (South Africa)	3110	(947)
Utigard Falls (Norway)	2625	(800)

Largest Islands

	Area	
	sq.mi.	(sq.km.)
Greenland	840,004	(2,175,601)
New Guinea	312,085	(800,510)
Borneo	292,000	(757,050)
Madagascar	226,658	(587,041)
Sumatra	202,300	(524,100)
Baffin Island	183,810	(476,065)
Great Britain	88,730	(229,870)
Honshu	88,031	(227,999)

Longest Rivers

	Length	
	mi.	(km.)
Nile (Africa)	4145	(6671)
Amazon (South America)	4050	(6515)
Yangtze (China)	3915	(6300)
Mississippi-Missouri-Red (North America)	3710	(5970)
Ob-Irtysh (Russia, Kazakhstan)	3460	(5570)
Yenisei (Russia)	3442	(5539)
Huang (Yellow River) (China)	3395	(5464)
Zaïre (Congo) (Africa)	2920	(4700)
Amur (Russia)	2744	(4416)
Lena (Russia)	2735	(4400)
Mackenzie-Peace (Canada)	2635	(4240)

Oceans

	Area		Greatest depth	
	sq.mi.	(sq.km.)	ft.	(m.)
Pacific	63,800,000	(165,240,000)	36,198	(11,033)
Atlantic	31,830,000	(82,439,355)	30,238	(9216)
Indian	28,900,000	(74,850,690)	25,344	(7725)
Arctic	5,500,000	(14,245,000)	18,050	(5500)

Highest Mountains

	Range	Height	
		ft.	(m.)
Mount Everest	Himalayas (China/Nepal)	29,028	(8848)
K2 (Godwin Austen)	Karakoram (China/India)	28,250	(8611)
Kanchenjunga	Himalayas (India/Nepal)	28,170	(8586)
Makalu 1	Himalayas (Nepal/China)	27,766	(8463)
Cho Oyu	Himalayas (Nepal/China)	26,906	(8201)
Dhaulagiri	Himalayas (Nepal)	26,795	(8167)
Manaslu	Himalayas (Nepal)	26,781	(8163)
Nanga Parbat	Himalayas (India)	26,660	(8126)

ARCTIC OCEAN

EUROPE

Alps Danube

Volga

Ob Siberia

Lena

Amur

Gobi

ASIA

Indus

Himalayas

Ganges

Yangtze

Sahara

Niger

Nile

AFRICA

Congo

PACIFIC OCEAN

INDIAN OCEAN

AUSTRALIA

SOUTHERN OCEAN

CLIMATE AND VEGETATION

The pattern of weather recorded at any one place over a long period is called the climate. The climate in Greenland, near the North Pole, is bitterly cold. The climate in equatorial Zaïre is warm and moist, or humid. The climate of a region is affected by its location on the planet, by its height above sea level, by its proximity to oceans or mountains, and by local winds. Different plants and animals are suited to different climates.

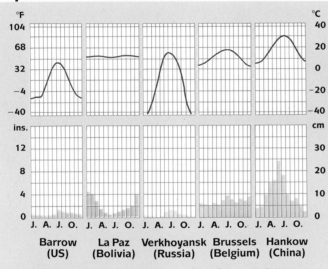

Barrow (US) | La Paz (Bolivia) | Verkhoyansk (Russia) | Brussels (Belgium) | Hankow (China)

For each climate station, the upper graph gives the average monthly temperature, the lower graph the average monthly rainfall. The color of the rainfall bars corresponds to the climatic zone in which the station is located, shown on the map.

Singapore | Williston (US) | Adelaide (Australia) | Minna (Nigeria) | Bahrain

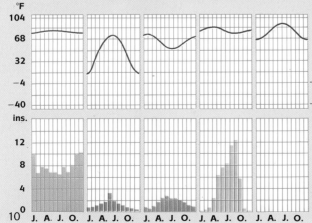

The world's "biomes"

A climatic zone which is home to certain kinds of creatures and plants is called a "biome." The diagrams on the left show the rainfall and temperature range of ten different biomes. These are keyed into the map on the right.

1 Tundra Treeless plain, frozen for much of the year, covered in grasses, mosses and low plants.

2 Mountains Dwarf shrubs and alpine plants provide low cover above the treeline.

3 Taiga Evergreen trees and shrubs which keep their leaves all the year round.

4 Temperate deciduous forest A milder climate produces trees which shed their leaves in Fall, such as oak and maple.

5 Temperate rainforest A mild, rainy climate favors ferns, mosses and tall treetops.

6 Tropical rainforest A warm, humid climate produces a dense tangle of vegetation and trees.

7 Temperate grassland Rolling grassy plains, prairies, or steppes, cover much of central Asia now, and at one time much of the United States and Canada.

8 Scrub Open bush country with thorn, shrubs or grassland.

9 Savanna The burning hot plains of central Africa are covered in coarse grasses and scattered trees.

10 Desert Sand and rock with little water. Home to tough plants such as cacti.

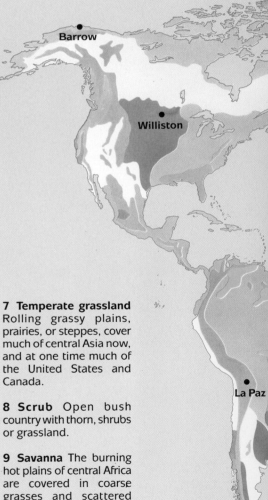

Temperature and rainfall

Water from the world's lakes and oceans evaporates, or turns into vapor. This rises into the air, and cools to form drops which fall as rain or snow. The world's pattern of winds is caused by the differences in temperature between the Poles and the Tropics.

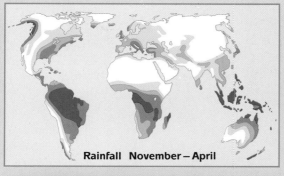

Rainfall November – April

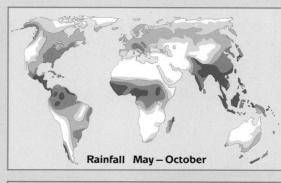

Rainfall May – October

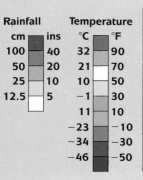

Rainfall		Temperature	
cm	ins	°C	°F
100	40	32	90
50	20	21	70
25	10	10	50
12.5	5	−1	30
		11	10
		−23	−10
		−34	−30
		−46	−50

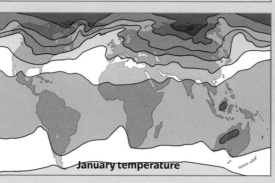

January temperature

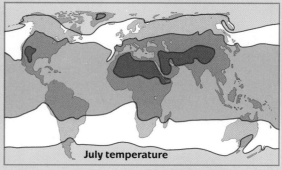

July temperature

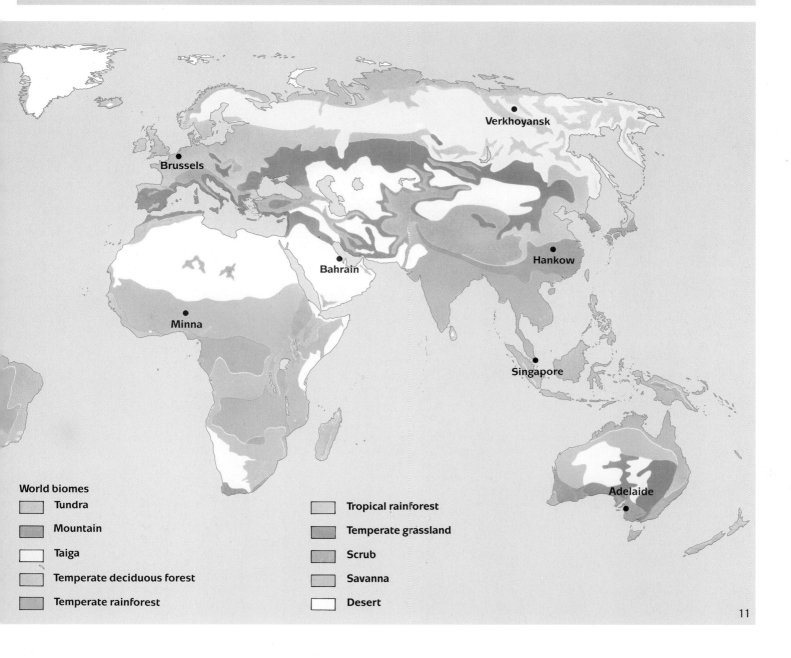

World biomes

- Tundra
- Mountain
- Taiga
- Temperate deciduous forest
- Temperate rainforest
- Tropical rainforest
- Temperate grassland
- Scrub
- Savanna
- Desert

11

WORLD ANIMALS

Over millions of years many different kinds, or species, of creatures have developed on Earth, from the great whales of the oceans to the elephants of the African plains. Insects are the most numerous creatures on Earth. Humans are the most intelligent species, but their activities now threaten the survival of much of the world's wildlife.

Sea otter

The world's animals
The 4230 species of mammal include whales, lions and tigers, monkeys, and humans. There are more than 8000 bird species, most of which can fly. Unlike birds and mammals, reptiles cannot control their own body temperature. There are more than 5000 species including snakes, lizards, crocodiles, and turtles. The 2500 amphibians include frogs, toads and newts. Fish number over 30,000 species.

All these creatures have bodies supported by skeletons. They are far outnumbered by invertebrates, or spineless animals. These include insects, worms, spiders, crabs, and shellfish.

Marine iguana

The world's oceans
The Blue whale is the largest animal on Earth. It feeds upon small shrimps called krill. The seas support a great wealth of animal life, including mammals such as the whales and dolphins, thousands of species of fish, seabirds, seals and sea lions, squid, octopus, sponges, corals, and jellyfish.

South America
The huge wings of the Andean condor help it to soar high above the South American peaks. The mountains are also inhabited by llamas and alpacas, members of the camel family, used for carrying goods and shorn for their wool. Monkeys, parrots, and giant snakes live deep in the rainforests of the Amazon.

Arctic tern

Harp seal

Moose

Chipmunk

Beaver

Prairie dog

Elf owl

Monarch butterfly

Roadrunner

Manatee

North America
The American Arctic is home to polar bears and seals. The great forests of Canada and Alaska are inhabited by moose, the largest deer in the world. The grasslands or prairies were once roamed by vast herds of bison (also called buffalo). Some have survived despite being hunted to the verge of extinction in the nineteenth century.

Condor

Armadillo

Toucan

Torrent duck

Giant anteater

Vicuña

Amazon river dolphin

Blue whale

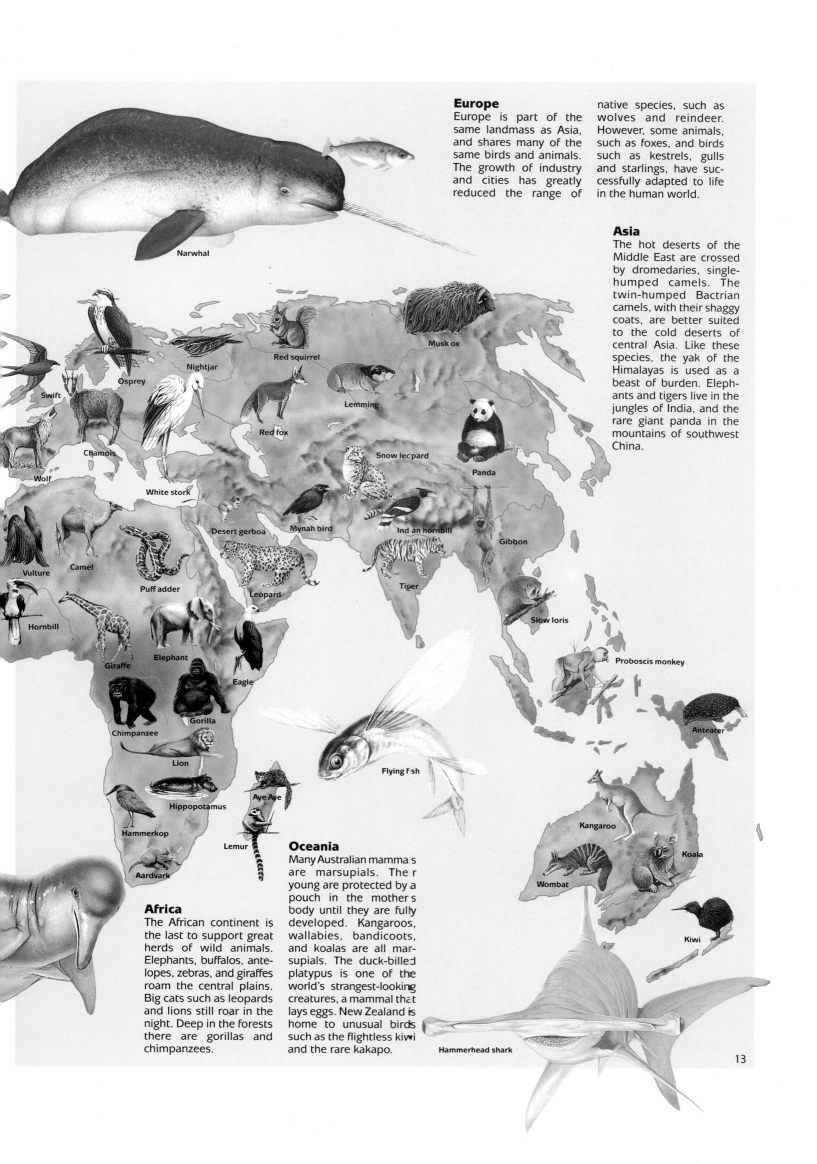

Europe

Europe is part of the same landmass as Asia, and shares many of the same birds and animals. The growth of industry and cities has greatly reduced the range of native species, such as wolves and reindeer. However, some animals, such as foxes, and birds such as kestrels, gulls and starlings, have successfully adapted to life in the human world.

Asia

The hot deserts of the Middle East are crossed by dromedaries, single-humped camels. The twin-humped Bactrian camels, with their shaggy coats, are better suited to the cold deserts of central Asia. Like these species, the yak of the Himalayas is used as a beast of burden. Elephants and tigers live in the jungles of India, and the rare giant panda in the mountains of southwest China.

Africa

The African continent is the last to support great herds of wild animals. Elephants, buffalos, antelopes, zebras, and giraffes roam the central plains. Big cats such as leopards and lions still roar in the night. Deep in the forests there are gorillas and chimpanzees.

Oceania

Many Australian mammals are marsupials. Their young are protected by a pouch in the mothers body until they are fully developed. Kangaroos, wallabies, bandicoots, and koalas are all marsupials. The duck-billed platypus is one of the world's strangest-looking creatures, a mammal that lays eggs. New Zealand is home to unusual birds such as the flightless kiwi and the rare kakapo.

Narwhal

Osprey

Swift

Nightjar

Red squirrel

Musk ox

Chamois

Lemming

Wolf

Red fox

White stork

Snow leopard

Panda

Desert gerboa

Mynah bird

Indian hornbill

Gibbon

Vulture

Camel

Puff adder

Leopard

Tiger

Slow loris

Hornbill

Giraffe

Elephant

Eagle

Proboscis monkey

Chimpanzee

Gorilla

Anteater

Lion

Flying fish

Aye Aye

Hippopotamus

Kangaroo

Hammerkop

Lemur

Koala

Aardvark

Wombat

Kiwi

Hammerhead shark

WORLD NATIONS

There are 229 countries in the world. Of these, 184 are independent nations, governing themselves. The rest are territories ruled or governed by other countries. Various peoples may live within the borders of a single country and some nations are made up of unions of smaller countries or states.

Countries are organized and governed in many different ways. Monarchies are ruled by kings or queens. Republics are headed by an elected president. Many countries have democratic governments, in which representatives are elected by the people. The elected representatives make up national assemblies, congresses, or "parliaments."

COUNTRY FACTS

The largest countries of the world

Country	Area sq.mi.	(Area sq.km)
Russia	6,593,391	(17,076,223)
Canada	3,851,810	(9,976,139)
China	3,695,500	(9,571,300)
U.S.A.	3,618,700	(9,372,570)
Brazil	3,286,488	(8,511,965)
Australia	2,966,151	(7,628,300)
India	1,269,350	(3,287,590)
Argentina	1,068,302	(2,766,889)
Kazakhstan	1,048,000	(2,714,215)
Sudan	967,500	(2,505,813)

The smallest countries of the world (excluding dependencies)

	Area sq.mi.	(Area sq.km)
Vatican City	0.17	(0.44)
Monaco	0.65	(1.6)
Nauru	8.2	(21.3)
Tuvalu	9.5	(24.6)
San Marino	23.4	(60.5)
Liechtenstein	62	(160)
Malta	122	(316)
Grenada	133	(345)
St. Vincent & the Grenadines	150	(388)
Barbados	166	(430)
Antigua & Barbuda	171	(442)
Andorra	180	(465)

The most populous countries of the world

Country	Population
China	1,072,330,000
India	853,400,000
U.S.A.	251,400,000
Indonesia	189,400,000
Brazil	150,400,000
Russia	148,900,000
Japan	123,600,000
Nigeria	118,800,000
Pakistan	114,600,000
Bangladesh	102,563,000

1 Denmark
2 Netherlands
3 Belgium
4 Luxembourg
5 Switzerland
6 Austria
7 Czechoslovakia
8 Hungary
9 Albania
10 Cyprus
11 Lebanon
12 Israel
13 Kuwait
14 Qatar
15 Brunei
16 Singapore
17 Togo
18 Benin
19 Equatorial Guinea
20 Rwanda
21 Burundi
22 Georgia
23 Armenia
24 Azerbaijan
25 Tajikistan
26 Moldova

The United Nations flag

United Nations

Many independent nations join together with others in order to form international groupings such as the European Community, the Caribbean Community, the League of Arab States, or the Organization of African Unity.

The largest international organization of all is made up of 166 countries. This is the United Nations Organization, founded by 50 countries in 1945. These founder members wished to ensure a peaceful future for the world.

The United Nations (U.N.) has not always been able to prevent war either, but it has helped to solve some of the world's problems. Member nations have sent troops in U.N. uniform to various trouble spots around the world.

The head of the United Nations is called the Secretary General. Delegates from all the member nations meet each year at the General Assembly, held at the organization's headquarters in New York City.

Fifteen nations form the Security Council, which meets to discuss crises and policy. Five nations — U.S., U.K., Russia, France, and China — are permanent members. Each of the other ten is elected by the General Assembly for a two-year term.

Some of the most important work of the U.N. is carried out by its agencies. These bodies deal with working conditions, food and agriculture, world health, finance, trade, communications, education, science, and culture.

WORLD POPULATION

In most countries, a census is taken every ten years or so, from which governments can count the number of people living within their borders. Population figures are important, for they help in the planning of housing, education, health care, and agriculture. Organizing a census can be very difficult in some parts of the world, where people live in remote deserts or mountains. China alone has a population of more than one billion, the world's highest.

About 5.5 billion people live in the world today, and about 180 babies are born every minute of the day. Such a vast number of people need enough food to stay alive and healthy. In the world's richer countries there is often too much food, which goes to waste. In the poorer regions of the world, food shortages and undernourishment are common.

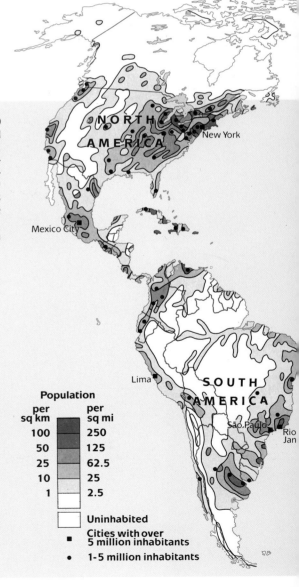

The population of the world

Our planet has become very crowded. In poor countries, many people move into the big cities in search of work. Other countries are filled with refugees, people fleeing from war or famine in neighboring lands. In the territory of Macao, on the south coast of China, there are over 65,000 people per square mile of land. Of the larger nations, Bangladesh has 1844 people per square mile. This compares with a population density of 918 per square mile in the Netherlands, and 68 in the United States. Greenland has only one person for every 10 square miles of land, and Antarctica is uninhabited, except by visiting scientists. The map of population density *(right)* shows that the world's most crowded places lie in the Far East, India, Europe, and the Eastern U.S.

The largest cities in the world

City	Population
Mexico City	18,748,000
São Paulo	10,063,110
Seoul	9,645,824
Calcutta	9,166,000
Moscow	8,967,000
Bombay	8,202,000
Tokyo	8,155,781
New York	7,262,700
Shanghai	7,180,000
London	6,770,400
Jakarta	6,503,449
Cairo	6,325,000
Delhi	6,220,000
Tehran	6,022,029
Beijing (Peking)	5,970,000
Bangkok	5,609,352
Rio de Janeiro	5,603,388
Istanbul	5,475,982
Tianjin	5,460,000
Karachi	5,103,000
Lima	5,008,400
St. Petersburg (Leningrad)	5,020,000
Shenyang	4,290,000
Madras	4,277,000
Bogotá	4,185,174
Toronto	3,427,168
Los Angeles	3,259,340
Wuhan	3,230,000
Yokohama	3,121,601
Chicago	3,009,530

Population

per sq km	per sq mi
100	250
50	125
25	62.5
10	25
1	2.5

Uninhabited

■ Cities with over 5 million inhabitants

● 1-5 million inhabitants

World population growth

In 1975 the population of the world was four billion. By 1985 it had grown to five billion. The map on the right shows how the population grew over that period.

Ten thousand years ago, the world population stood at about five million. By the middle of the next century, it will have reached more than eight billion. This rapid growth in population is sometimes referred to as an "explosion." It has been caused by improvements in medicine and health care, in the growing of crops and the supply of food.

The rate of population growth is now slowing down, but the number of humans is still increasing by about 90 million every year.

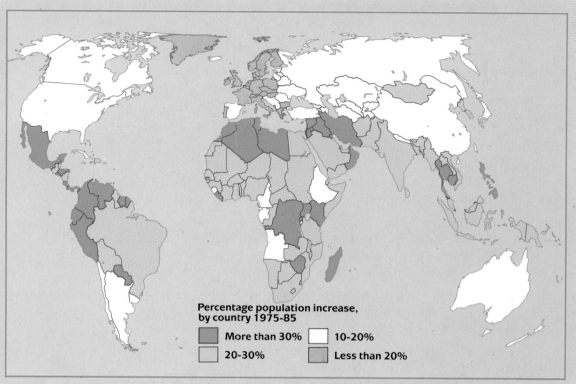

Percentage population increase, by country 1975-85

▨ More than 30%	☐ 10-20%
☐ 20-30%	▨ Less than 20%

LANGUAGES AND RELIGIONS

Each continent is home to many different peoples. All share common concerns and interests, whatever the color of their skin, or their religious or political beliefs.

The way of life followed by any one group of people is called a culture. There is a rich variety of cultures in the world today. Despite a world-wide system of communications, people have not adopted identical ways of life. They are proud of their historical backgrounds and their regional customs. There are often many different cultures within a single country; for example, 56 ethnic groups live within China alone.

About 5000 languages are spoken around the world, and they are written down in a number of different alphabets and symbols. Many languages have regional variants, or dialects.

Languages of the world

Language	Estimated number of speakers
Mandarin (Chinese)	844,000,000
English	437,000,000
Hindi	338,000,000
Spanish	331,000,000
Russian	291,000,000
Arabic	192,000,000
Bengali	181,000,000
Portuguese	171,000,000
Malay-Indonesian	138,000,000
Japanese	124,000,000
French	119,000,000
German	118,000,000

Religions of the world

Major religions	Estimated number of followers
Christianity	1,670,000,000
(Roman Catholic)	952,000,000
(Protestant)	337,000,000
(Orthodox)	162,000,000
Islam	881,000,000
Hinduism	663,000,000
Buddhism	312,000,000
Judaism	18,000,000
Sikhism	17,000,000
Confucianism	6,000,000
Baha'ism	5,000,000
Jainism	4,000,000
Shintoism	3,000,000
(Chinese folk religions)	172,000,000
(Tribal religions)	92,000,000
(Atheists)	230,000,000

NORTH AMERICA

SOUTH AMERICA

Language families

Indo-European
- Germanic
- Romance
- Slav
- Baltic
- Greek
- Albanian
- Armenian
- Iranian
- Hindi

Altaic
- Turkic
- Mongolian
- Korean

Religions and beliefs

From earliest times, humans have tried to find out the meaning of their lives and of the world around them. People have worshipped the Sun and Moon, the natural world, and all kinds of spirits, gods and goddesses. Three great faiths were born in the deserts of the Middle East: the followers of Judaism, Christianity, and Islam all believe in a single God. India saw the rise of Hinduism, Buddhism, and Sikhism. Taoism and Confucianism began in China, and Shinto in Japan. Atheism is the belief that there is no God.

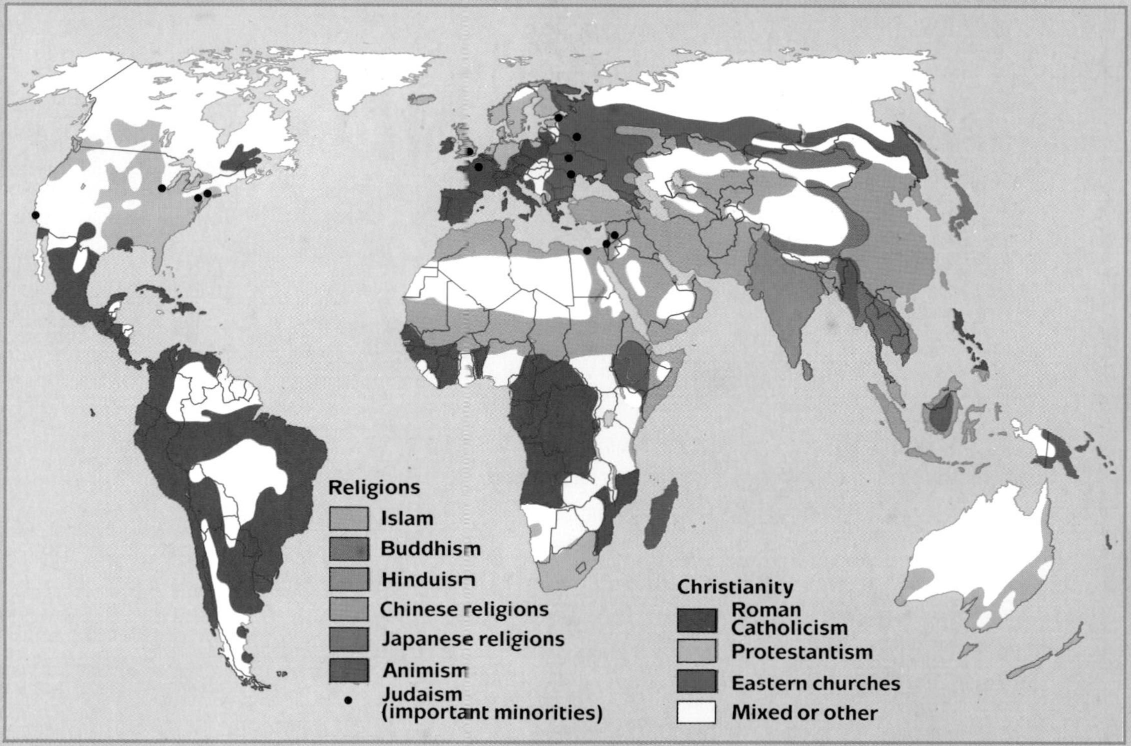

Religions

- Islam
- Buddhism
- Hinduism
- Chinese religions
- Japanese religions
- Animism
- • Judaism (important minorities)

Christianity

- Roman Catholicism
- Protestantism
- Eastern churches
- Mixed or other

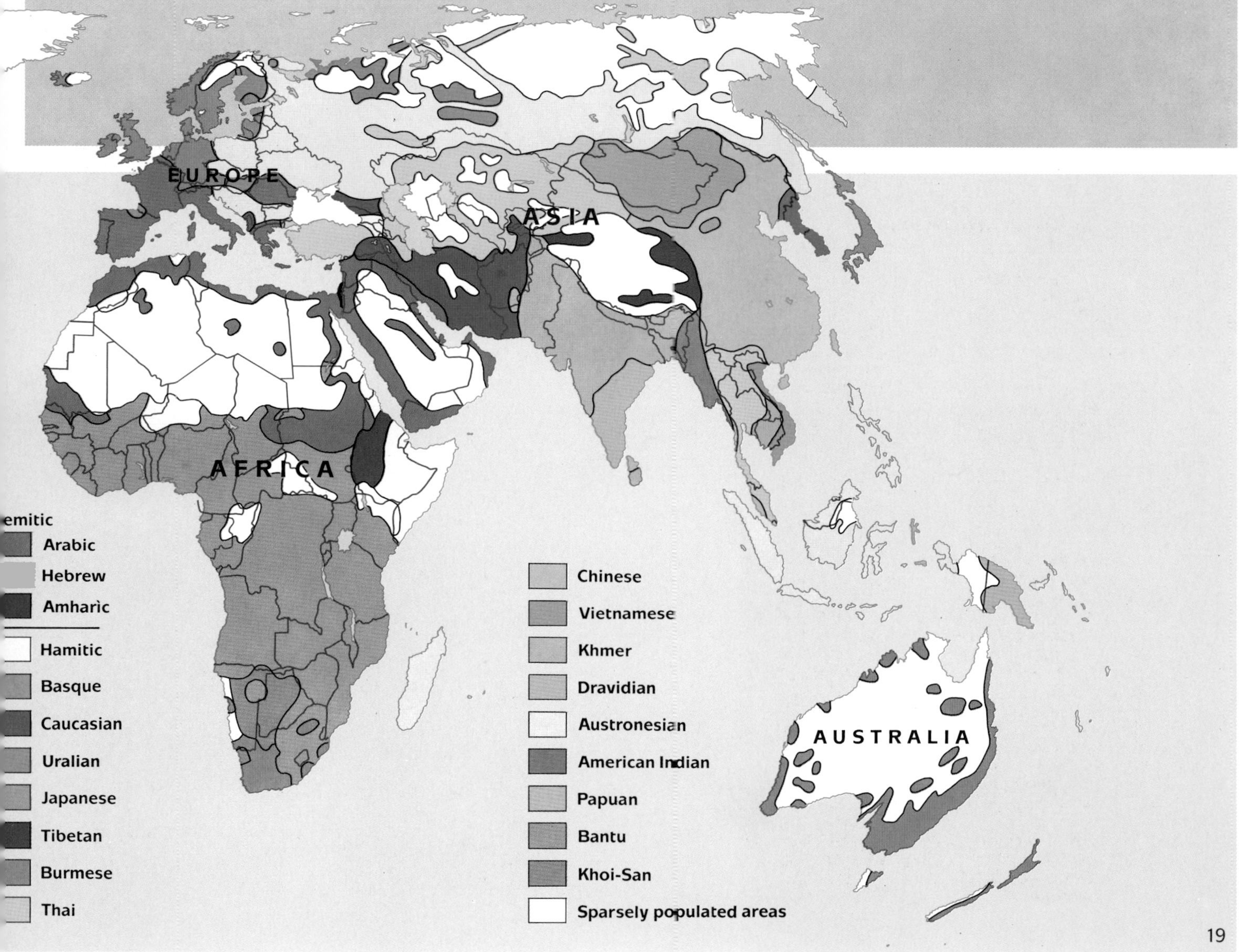

EUROPE

ASIA

AFRICA

AUSTRALIA

Semitic
- Arabic
- Hebrew
- Amharic

- Hamitic
- Basque
- Caucasian
- Uralian
- Japanese
- Tibetan
- Burmese
- Thai

- Chinese
- Vietnamese
- Khmer
- Dravidian
- Austronesian
- American Indian
- Papuan
- Bantu
- Khoi-San
- Sparsely populated areas

LAND USE AND AGRICULTURE

The first humans lived by gathering wild nuts and berries, by hunting, and by fishing. Ten thousand years of farming have seen the clearing of the world's great forests and the cultivation of former grasslands. The growing of basic foodstuffs, or staple crops, is vital to feed the world's hungry mouths. Modern methods have enabled richer countries to produce more food than they need, while in poor countries the opposite is often true.

Each pie diagram shows how total world production is shared between the top producers listed below.

* Based on production figures issued before the independence of former Soviet republics in 1991.

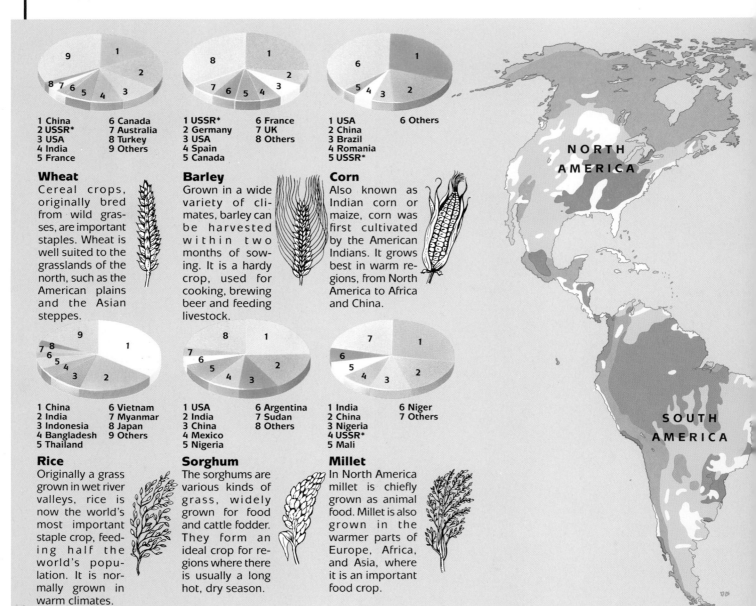

1 China	6 Canada
2 USSR*	7 Australia
3 USA	8 Turkey
4 India	9 Others
5 France	

Wheat
Cereal crops, originally bred from wild grasses, are important staples. Wheat is well suited to the grasslands of the north, such as the American plains and the Asian steppes.

1 USSR*	6 France
2 Germany	7 UK
3 USA	8 Others
4 Spain	
5 Canada	

Barley
Grown in a wide variety of climates, barley can be harvested within two months of sowing. It is a hardy crop, used for cooking, brewing beer and feeding livestock.

1 USA	6 Others
2 China	
3 Brazil	
4 Romania	
5 USSR*	

Corn
Also known as Indian corn or maize, corn was first cultivated by the American Indians. It grows best in warm regions, from North America to Africa and China.

1 China	6 Vietnam
2 India	7 Myanmar
3 Indonesia	8 Japan
4 Bangladesh	9 Others
5 Thailand	

Rice
Originally a grass grown in wet river valleys, rice is now the world's most important staple crop, feeding half the world's population. It is normally grown in warm climates.

1 USA	6 Argentina
2 India	7 Sudan
3 China	8 Others
4 Mexico	
5 Nigeria	

Sorghum
The sorghums are various kinds of grass, widely grown for food and cattle fodder. They form an ideal crop for regions where there is usually a long hot, dry season.

1 India	6 Niger
2 China	7 Others
3 Nigeria	
4 USSR*	
5 Mali	

Millet
In North America millet is chiefly grown as animal food. Millet is also grown in the warmer parts of Europe, Africa, and Asia, where it is an important food crop.

NORTH AMERICA

SOUTH AMERICA

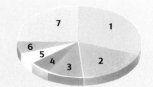

1 India	6 Indonesia
2 China	7 Others
3 Sri Lanka	
4 Kenya	
5 Turkey	

1 Brazil	6 Ethiopia
2 Colombia	7 Uganda
3 Mexico	8 Indonesia
4 El Salvador	9 Others
5 Guatemala	

1 China	6 Others
2 USA	
3 India	
4 Pakistan	
5 Brazil	

1 Italy	6 Others
2 France	
3 Spain	
4 Argentina	
5 USA	

1 Malaysia	
2 Indonesia	
3 Thailand	
4 Others	

Tea

The mountainous regions of China, India and Sri Lanka are suitable for growing tea. This tropical ever- green shrub needs a fertile soil and a warm, rainy cli- mate. It prefers higher elevations and is grown on terraced hills.

Coffee

This small tree was first grown in Africa. It was later introduced from Arabia to Java, the Caribbean, Brazil, and India. Its red berries contain two hard beans. These are roasted and ground into a powder.

Cotton

Inside the seed heads, or bolls, of the cotton shrub is a mass of white fibers up to two inches long. These are cleaned and untangled, spun into yarn and woven into cloth. Cotton is grown in many warm lands around the world.

Grapes

Vines are grown for their grapes, which are eaten fresh or dried to make raisins. Many are pressed, and the juice is fermented, a pro- cess which turns the grape sugar into alcohol. Grape vines are grown on sunny hillsides.

Rubber

The commerical or Pará rubber tree is a native of Brazil which was later introduced to Southeast Asia. When the trunk is cut, a milky white gum oozes out to protect the tree. This substance, called latex, is processed to make rubber.

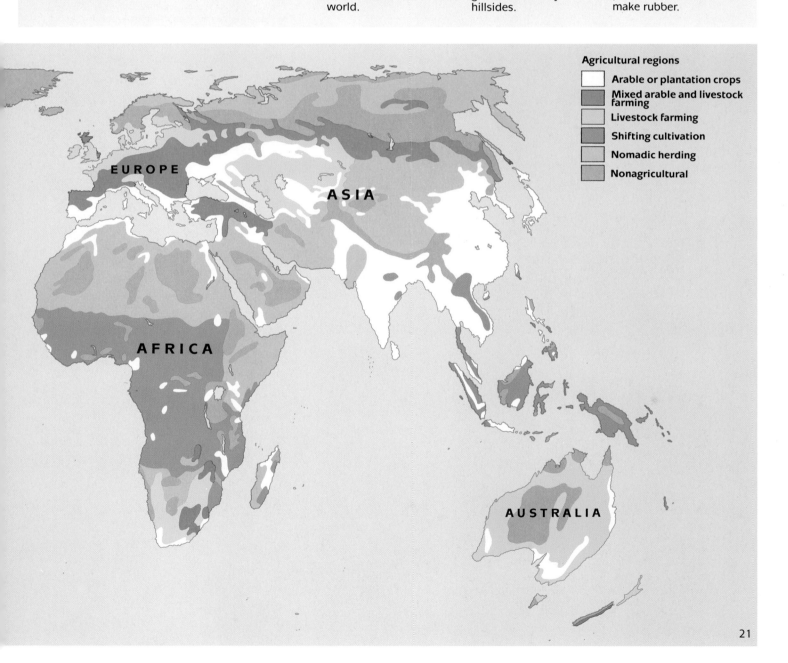

Agricultural regions

- Arable or plantation crops
- Mixed arable and livestock farming
- Livestock farming
- Shifting cultivation
- Nomadic herding
- Nonagricultural

EUROPE

ASIA

AFRICA

AUSTRALIA

MINERALS AND INDUSTRY

Beneath the surface of the Earth lies a wealth of minerals. These include ores, or rocks which contain metals, and fuels such as coal, oil, or natural gas. Manufacturing industries use energy and raw materials to produce goods. Countries rich in these natural resources can build up their manufacturing industries, or increase their wealth by selling the minerals to other countries. Countries lacking in natural resources must import them.

Each pie diagram shows how total world production is shared between the top producers listed below.

* Based on production figures issued before the independence of former Soviet republics in 1991.

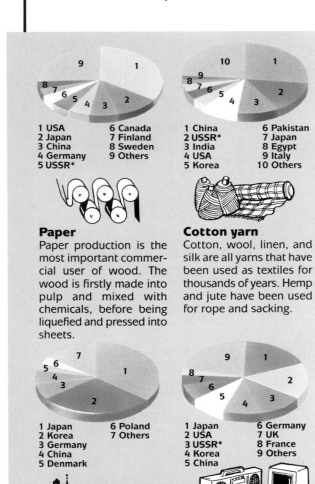

1 USA	6 Canada
2 Japan	7 Finland
3 China	8 Sweden
4 Germany	9 Others
5 USSR*	

Paper
Paper production is the most important commercial user of wood. The wood is firstly made into pulp and mixed with chemicals, before being liquefied and pressed into sheets.

1 China	6 Pakistan
2 USSR*	7 Japan
3 India	8 Egypt
4 USA	9 Italy
5 Korea	10 Others

Cotton yarn
Cotton, wool, linen, and silk are all yarns that have been used as textiles for thousands of years. Hemp and jute have been used for rope and sacking.

1 USSR*	6 Italy
2 Japan	7 Brazil
3 USA	8 France
4 China	9 Others
5 Germany	

Steel
Steel is made from iron mixed with carbon. Nickel, chromium, tungsten, cobalt, or other metals are added if the steel is to be stainless, or very strong.

1 Japan	6 Poland
2 Korea	7 Others
3 Germany	
4 China	
5 Denmark	

Shipbuilding
A decline in world shipping has closed shipyards around the world. However, the oil industry has provided work, with orders for drilling rigs and supertankers (giant carriers of crude oil).

1 Japan	6 Germany
2 USA	7 UK
3 USSR*	8 France
4 Korea	9 Others
5 China	

Electronic goods
Radios, cassette players, stereos, video recorders, television sets, compact disc systems, home computers, and calculators are the basis of today's vast electronic goods industry.

1 Japan	6 Spain
2 USA	7 USSR*
3 Germany	8 UK
4 France	9 Others
5 Italy	

Cars
Invented in Europe, the automobile was first mass-produced in the United States, by Henry Ford (1863-1947). The automobile revolutionized transportation and daily life.

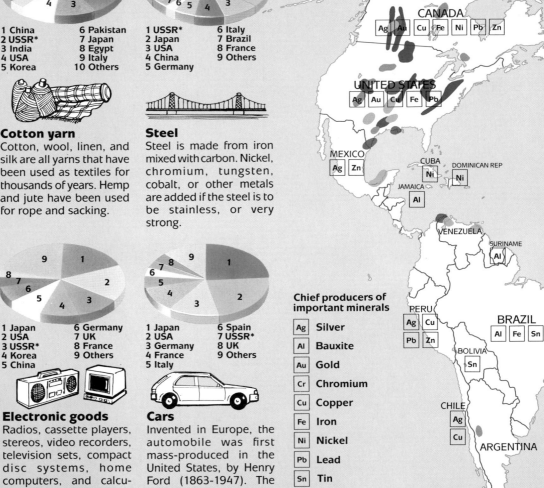

Chief producers of important minerals

Ag	Silver
Al	Bauxite
Au	Gold
Cr	Chromium
Cu	Copper
Fe	Iron
Ni	Nickel
Pb	Lead
Sn	Tin
Zn	Zinc
◆	Diamonds

1 USSR*   **6 Iran**
2 USA   **7 Iraq**
3 Saudi Arabia   **8 Canada**
4 Mexico   **9 Venezuela**
5 China   **10 Others**

1 USSR*   **6 USA**
2 Brazil   **7 Canada**
3 Australia   **8 Others**
4 China
5 India

1 Chile   **6 Zambia**
2 USA·   **7 Poland**
3 Canada   **8 Peru**
4 USSR*   **9 Australia**
5 Zaïre   **10 Others**

1 Australia   **6 Yugoslavia**
2 Guinea   **7 Others**
3 Jamaica
4 Brazil
5 USSR*

1 Malaysia   **6 China**
2 Brazil   **7 Bolivia**
3 USSR*   **8 Australia**
4 Indonesia   **9 Others**
5 Thailand

Oil

Oil, or petroleum, is found under the ground or beneath the seabed and is raised by drilling. It is then refined for use as fuel, or processed and made into plastics, waxes, paints, and synthetic fibers. Oil and gas provide around three quarters of the world's energy.

Iron ore

This metal ore is mined in the Soviet Union, Australia, the United States and many other parts of the world. The ore is crushed, sorted, and transported to a furnace, where it is burned at high temperatures to make steel.

Copper

Copper is used in telecommunications, heating and electrical systems, and many other areas of industry. It can be alloyed, or combined, with tin to produce bronze, and with tin, zinc and copper to produce brass.

Bauxite

Bauxite is the name of the ore that contains aluminium, a lightweight metal used widely in industry and shaped into cans, strips and wires. It is mined in the Caribbean, in Europe, Australia, and the Soviet Union.

Tin

Tin is widely used by the world's industrial nations. It is added to other metals to make alloys such as bronze, and used for coating steel to prevent rusting. Tin is mined in South America, Southeast Asia, China, the Soviet Union, and Australia.

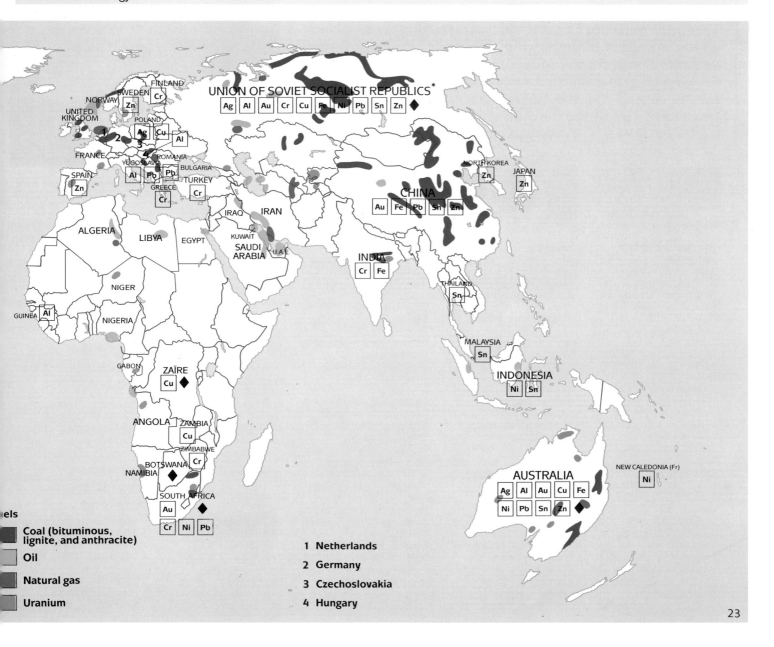

els

■ **Coal (bituminous, lignite, and anthracite)**
□ **Oil**
■ **Natural gas**
□ **Uranium**

1 Netherlands
2 Germany
3 Czechoslovakia
4 Hungary

23

NORTH AMERICA

North America stretches from the Arctic icecap to the tropical shores of the Caribbean Sea. It includes two of the largest countries in the world, the United States and Canada, and some of the smallest, the tiny island nations of the Caribbean. From Vancouver to St. John's, Newfoundland, the continent measures over 3000 miles across.

The immensely varied landscape includes the tundra and forests of northern Canada, the vast, featureless croplands of the American Midwest, the deserts of northern Mexico and the rainforests of Central America. Running the length of its western side is North America's mountainous backbone. In this region lie the spectacular peaks of the Rocky Mountains, the Grand Canyon, and, in Central America, the active volcanoes of Guatemala, El Salvador, and Nicaragua.

The Niagara Falls, which lie between Lake Erie and Lake Ontario.

North America
Highest point Mount McKinley (Alaska, U.S.A.) 20,320ft. (6194m.)
Lowest point Death Valley (California, U.S.A.) 282ft. (86m.)
Longest river Mississippi-Missouri-Red (U.S.A.) 3710mi. (5970 km.)
Largest lake Superior (U.S.A./Canada) 31,795 sq.mi. (82,348 sq.km.)

UNITED STATES OF AMERICA
Area 3,618,700 sq. miles (9,372,570 sq. km.)
Population 251,400,000
Capital Washington, D.C. (pop. 638,432)
Largest cities New York (7,262,700)
Los Angeles (3,259,340)
Chicago (3,009,530)
Houston (1,728,910)
Philadelphia (1,642,900)
Detroit (1,086,220)
San Diego (1,015,190)
Dallas (1,003,520)
Currency US dollar
Official language(s) English
Chief products Wheat, corn, soybeans, minerals, machinery, oil, natural gas, iron and steel
Exports Machinery, vehicles, cereals, chemicals, crude materials
Imports Machinery, vehicles, manufactured goods, food (fish and vegetables) oil

CANADA
Area 3,851,810 sq. miles (9,976,139 sq. km.)
Population 26,600,000
Capital Ottawa (pop. 300,763)
Largest cities Toronto (3,427,168)
Montréal (2,921,357)
Vancouver (1,380,729)
Edmonton (785,465)
Calgary (671,326)
Currency Canadian dollar
Official language(s) English and French
Chief products Wheat, minerals, furs, lumber, fish, oil, natural gas
Exports Machinery, paper, vehicles, lumber, metals (especially aluminum, nickel, uranium)
Imports Machinery, food, vehicles, chemicals, iron and steel, oil

GREENLAND (Denmark)
Area 840,004 sq. miles (2,175,601 sq. km.)
Population 53,406
Capital Godthåb

MEXICO
Official name Estados Unidos Mexicanos
Area 761,610 sq. miles (1,972,547 sq. km.)
Population 86,800,000
Capital Mexico City (pop. 18,748,000)
Largest cities Guadalajara (2,578,000)
Monterrey (2,335,000)
Puebla (1,217,600)
León (946,800)
Torreón (729,800)
Currency Mexican peso
Official language(s) Spanish (Amerindian languages are also spoken)
Chief products Oil, iron and steel, minerals (especially gold and silver), corn, sorghum, oranges
Exports Oil, manufactured goods, machinery, minerals, textiles, coffee
Imports Vehicles, industrial machinery (motor pumps, textile machinery), food (corn and soy beans)

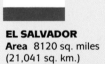

GUATEMALA
Area 42,040 sq. miles (108,889 sq. km.)
Population 9,200,000
Capital Guatemala City
Chief products Coffee, cotton, chemicals, bananas, corn, sugarcane

EL SALVADOR
Area 8120 sq. miles (21,041 sq. km.)
Population 5,300,000
Capital San Salvador
Chief products Coffee, textiles, sugarcane, corn

NICARAGUA
Area 57,130 sq. miles (148,000 sq. km.)
Population 3,900,000
Capital Managua
Chief products Coffee, cotton, sugar, shellfish

COSTA RICA
Area 19,600 sq. miles (50,700 sq. km.)
Population 2,990,000
Capital San José
Chief products Coffee, bananas, sugar, cocoa, cattle, manufactured goods

NAME	AREA SQ. MILES (SQ. KM.)	POPULATION	CAPITAL
Anguilla (U.K.)	35 (91)	7000	The Valley
Antigua and Barbuda	171 (442)	81,000	St. John's
Aruba (Netherlands)	75 (193)	68,000	Oranjestad
Bahamas	5353 (13,864)	243,000	Nassau
Barbados	166 (430)	300,000	Bridgetown
Bermuda (U.K.)	21 (54)	57,145	Hamilton
British Virgin Islands (U.K.)	59 (153)	12,000	Road Town
Cayman Islands (U.K.)	100 (259)	22,000	Georgetown
Dominica	290 (752)	77,000	Roseau
Grenada	133 (345)	112,000	St. George's
Guadeloupe (Fr.)	657 (1702)	330,000	Basse-Terre
Martinique (Fr.)	417 (1079)	330,000	Fort-de-France
Montserrat (U.K.)	41 (106)	12,000	Plymouth
Netherlands Antilles (Netherlands)	383 (993)	261,850	Willemstad
St. Kitts (Christopher)-Nevis	101 (262)	46,000	Basseterre
St. Lucia	238 (616)	200,000	Castries
St. Vincent and the Grenadines	150 (388)	100,000	Kingstown
Trinidad and Tobago	1980 (5130)	1,204,000	Port of Spain
Turks and Caicos Is. (U.K.)	192 (430)	8000	Coburn Town
U.S. Virgin Islands (U.S.A.)	133 (345)	111,000	Charlotte Amalie
St. Pierre et Miquelon (Fr.)	93 (241)	6500	St. Pierre

ANTIGUA AND BARBUDA

BAHAMAS

BARBADOS

DOMINICA

GRENADA

ST. KITTS-NEVIS

ST. LUCIA

ST. VINCENT AND THE GRENADINES

TRINIDAD AND TOBAGO

U.S. VIRGIN ISLANDS

DOMINICAN REPUBLIC
Area 18,820 sq. miles
(48,374 sq. km.)
Population 7,200,000
Capital Santo Domingo
Chief products Sugar,
bauxite, silver, cocoa, coffee

JAMAICA
Area 4240 sq. miles
(10,991 sq. km.)
Population 2,470,000
Capital Kingston
Chief products Sugar,
bananas, alumina, bauxite

HAITI
Area 10,710 sq. miles
(27,750 sq. km.)
Population 6,500,000
Capital Port-au-Prince
Chief products Coffee, sisal,
manufactured goods, sugar

BELIZE
Area 8870 sq. miles
(22,963 sq. km.)
Population 200,000
Capital Belmopan
Chief products Fruit, fish,
vegetables, shellfish, lumber

HONDURAS
Area 43,280 sq. miles
(112,088 sq. km.)
Population 5,100,000
Capital Tegucigalpa
Chief products Bananas,
coffee, lumber, sugar,
tobacco

PANAMA
Area 29,670 sq. miles
(77,082 sq. km.)
Population 2,346,000
Capital Panamá
Chief products Bananas,
lumber, copper, rice, sugar

PUERTO RICO (U.S.A.)
Area 3520 sq. miles
(9104 sq. km.)
Population 3,301,000
Capital San Juan
Chief products
Manufactured goods, sugar-
cane, machinery, coffee

CUBA
Area 42,800 sq. miles
(110,861 sq. km.)
Population 10,600,000
Capital Havana
Chief products Sugar, oil,
minerals (nickel, iron ore),
rice, corn, coffee, tobacco

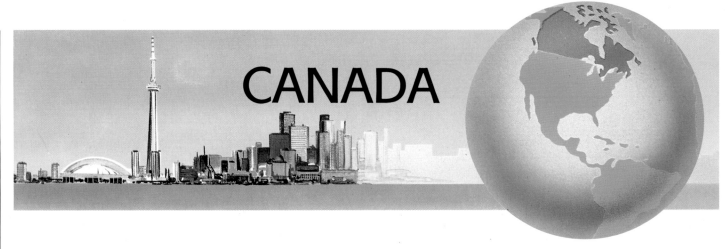

CANADA

C anada is the second largest country in the world, yet only 20 percent of it is inhabited. Much of its territory is either "tundra" (Arctic plains where the soil is permanently frozen) or forest. Most of the people live in the urban areas that hug the Great Lakes and the St. Lawrence Seaway, a major shipping route.

Canada has rich natural resources of minerals such as zinc, nickel, and uranium. Pulp and paper are made from the huge supplies of wood, while vast prairie lands make Canada one of the world's leading producers of wheat. Deep-sea fishing is important on the Atlantic coast of Canada: shellfish, lobsters, and cod are canned or frozen for export.

BEAUFORT SEA

Banks Isl

Dawson

Mackenzie Mountains

Mackenzie

Great Bear Lake

YUKON TERRITORY

▲ Mt Logan 19,850

Yukon

N O R T H

Whitehorse

Yellowkni

C

A

Rocky Mountains

Coast

PeC

Queen Charlotte Islands

B R I T I S H

Prince George

C O L U M B I A

A L B E

Mountains

Fraser

Edmonto

Vancouver I.

Calgary

Vancouver

Victoria

The Welland Canal
The Welland Canal connects two of the Great Lakes, Erie and Ontario.

It is deep enough for container ships, bound for the Atlantic Ocean via the St. Lawrence Seaway.

The Prairies
The plains of Alberta, Saskatchewan, and Manitoba in central Canada are known as "the Prairies."

Ice hockey
Ice hockey is Canada's national game. In winter it is popular with teams of young players, who can enjoy the sport in local outdoor or indoor rinks in most regions of the country.

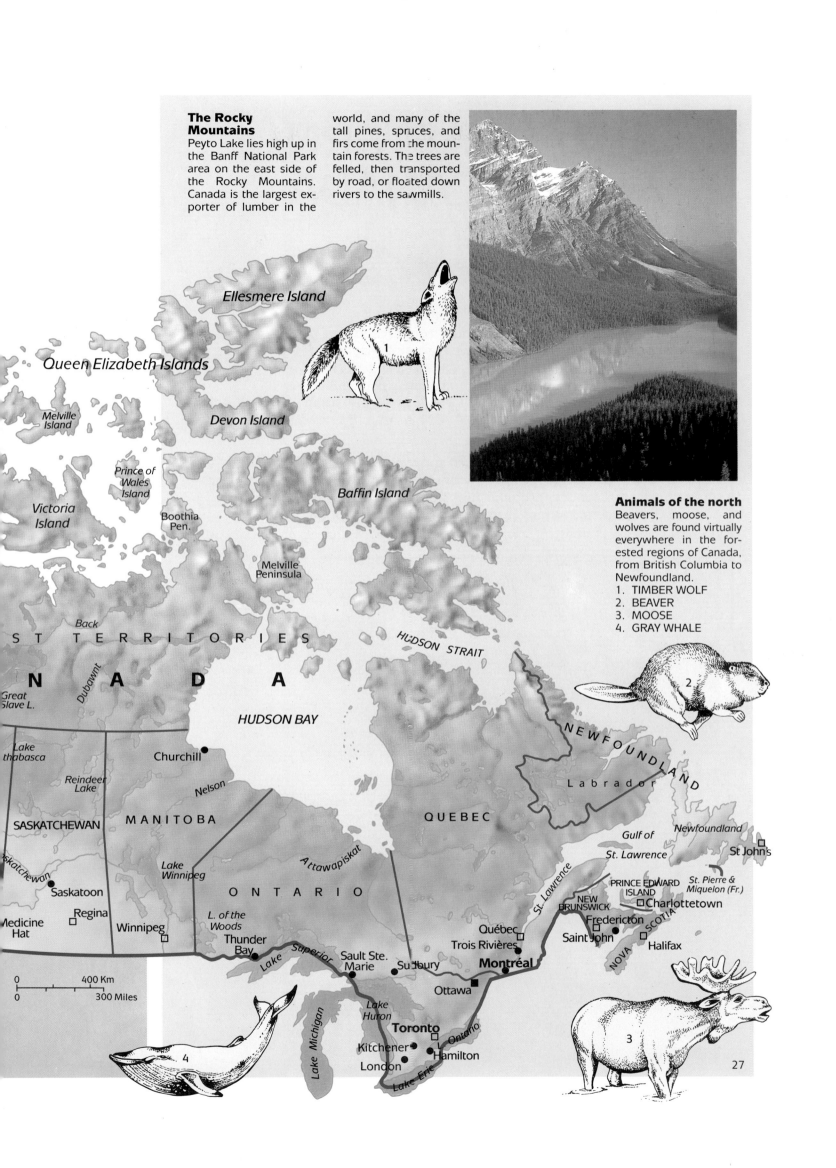

The Rocky Mountains
Peyto Lake lies high up in the Banff National Park area on the east side of the Rocky Mountains. Canada is the largest exporter of lumber in the world, and many of the tall pines, spruces, and firs come from the mountain forests. The trees are felled, then transported by road, or floated down rivers to the sawmills.

Animals of the north
Beavers, moose, and wolves are found virtually everywhere in the forested regions of Canada, from British Columbia to Newfoundland.
1. TIMBER WOLF
2. BEAVER
3. MOOSE
4. GRAY WHALE

Ellesmere Island

Queen Elizabeth Islands

Melville Island

Prince of Wales Island

Victoria Island

Devon Island

Boothia Pen.

Baffin Island

Melville Peninsula

ST   T E R R I T O R I E S

Back

N A D A

Dubawnt

Great Slave L.

HUDSON STRAIT

HUDSON BAY

NEWFOUNDLAND

Labrador

Lake Athabasca

Churchill

Reindeer Lake

Nelson

SASKATCHEWAN

MANITOBA

QUEBEC

Gulf of St. Lawrence

Newfoundland

St John's

Attawapiskat

St. Lawrence

PRINCE EDWARD ISLAND

St. Pierre & Miquelon (Fr.)

Lake Winnipeg

ONTARIO

NEW BRUNSWICK

Charlottetown

skatchewan

Saskatoon

L. of the Woods

Québec

Fredericton

Regina

Winnipeg

Thunder Bay

Trois Rivières

Saint John

NOVA SCOTIA

Halifax

Medicine Hat

Lake Superior

Sault Ste. Marie

Sudbury

Montréal

0   400 Km
0   300 Miles

Ottawa

Lake Huron

Lake Michigan

Toronto

L. Ontario

Kitchener

Hamilton

London

Lake Erie

27

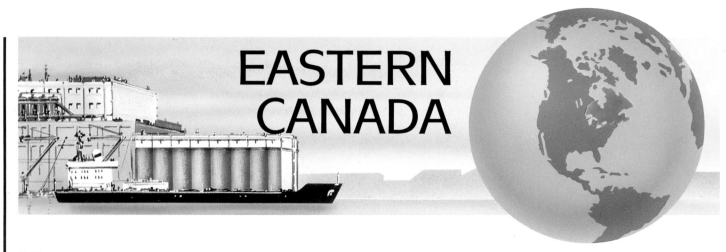

EASTERN CANADA

Eastern Canada is home to the Inuit, to descendants of French and British settlers, and to a growing population of immigrants from around the world. Canada's largest city is Toronto, a business center on Lake Ontario, with a metropolitan population of well over three million. Ottawa is the Canadian capital, and Montréal is the largest city in the French-speaking province of Québec.

The eastern cities are industrial, with supplies of oil piped from Alberta in the west. The St. Lawrence Seaway provides an important link for ocean-going ships between the Atlantic and the Great Lakes. Farming is important in the south of the region.

Agriculture in Québec
The region's farmland produces dairy products, cattle, pigs, poultry and corn.

Château Frontenac
Québec City's Château Frontenac Hotel was built by the Canadian Pacific Railway in 1892-3.

Mining
Canada is rich in minerals, producing copper, nickel, zinc, and iron ore.

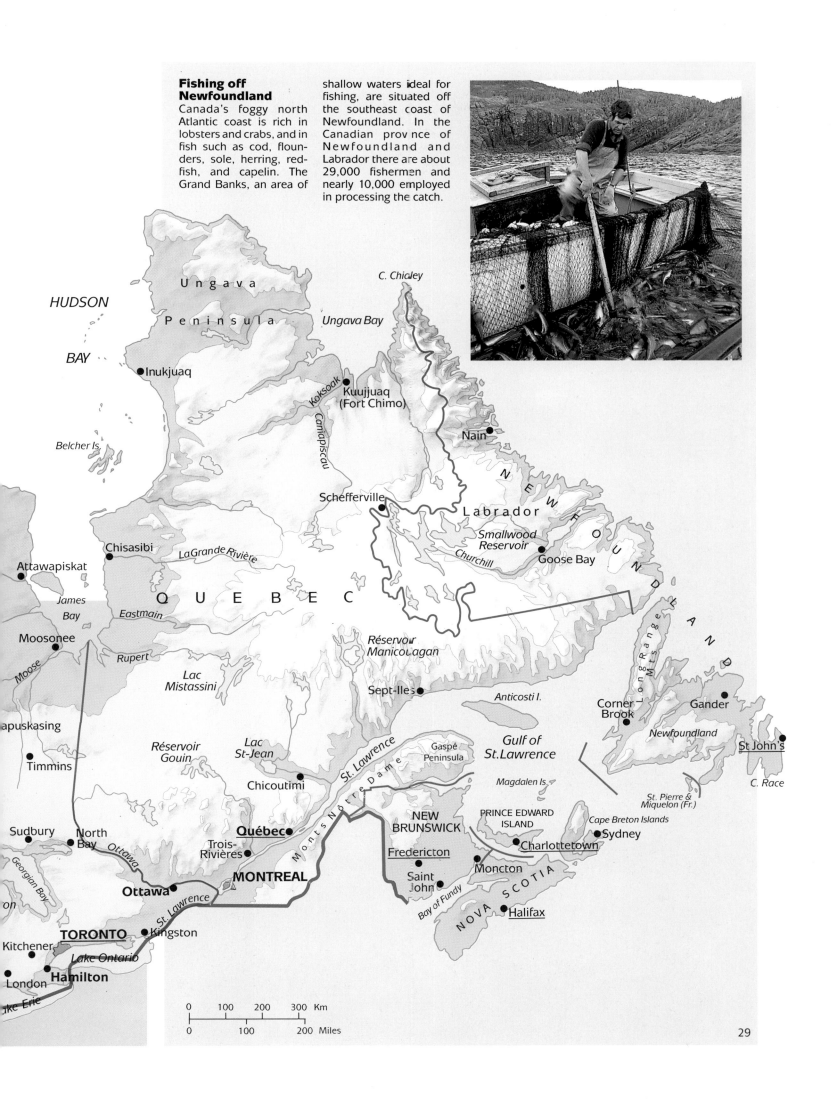

Fishing off Newfoundland
Canada's foggy north Atlantic coast is rich in lobsters and crabs, and in fish such as cod, flounders, sole, herring, redfish, and capelin. The Grand Banks, an area of shallow waters ideal for fishing, are situated off the southeast coast of Newfoundland. In the Canadian province of Newfoundland and Labrador there are about 29,000 fishermen and nearly 10,000 employed in processing the catch.

HUDSON

BAY

U n g a v a

P e n i n s u l a

Ungava Bay

C. Chidley

Inukjuaq

Belcher Is.

Koksoak

Kuujjuaq
(Fort Chimo)

Caniapiscau

Nain

N
E
W
F
O
U
N
D
L
A
N
D

Schefferville

Labrador

Chisasibi

LaGrande Rivière

Smallwood
Reservoir

Churchill

Goose Bay

Attawapiskat

James
Bay

Eastmain

Q U E B E C

Moosonee

Rupert

Réservoir
Manicouagan

Long Range Mts.

Moose

Lac
Mistassini

Sept-Iles

Anticosti I.

Corner
Brook

Gander

apuskasing

Réservoir
Gouin

Lac
St-Jean

Newfoundland

St John's

Timmins

Chicoutimi

St. Lawrence

Gaspé
Peninsula

Gulf of
St.Lawrence

C. Race

Sudbury

North
Bay

Ottawa

Monts Notre Dame

Québec

Trois-
Rivières

Magdalen Is.

PRINCE EDWARD
ISLAND

St. Pierre &
Miquelon (Fr.)

Cape Breton Islands

Sydney

Georgian Bay

MONTREAL

NEW
BRUNSWICK

Charlottetown

Ottawa

St. Lawrence

Fredericton

Moncton

N
O
V
A

S
C
O
T
I
A

TORONTO

Kingston

Saint
John

Kitchener

Lake Ontario

Bay of Fundy

Halifax

London

Hamilton

ke Erie

| 0 | 100 | 200 | 300 | Km |

| 0 | 100 | | 200 | Miles |

WESTERN CANADA

I n the west of Canada the province of British Columbia flanks the Pacific Ocean. The province includes not only the Pacific coastline but also the high peaks of the Rocky Mountains, as they begin their long march southwards, down the continent. The other western provinces of Alberta, Saskatchewan and Manitoba are sometimes called the "bread basket of the world" because of the wheat farms which stretch across their vast prairie lands. All three have more extreme climates than British Columbia, because they are far from the warming influence of the sea.

Canada's western provinces derive much of their wealth from lumber, ranching, agriculture, mining, and oil. The chief cities of western Canada are in the southern, more temperate regions of these huge territories. Winnipeg is a center of industry and grain trading. In Alberta, Edmonton is an oil town, and Calgary is famed for its ranching and rodeos. Vancouver is the major port of Canada's Pacific coast.

View over Vancouver
Sea and mountains provide a beautiful setting for Canada's third biggest city (after Toronto and Montréal). Vancouver is a major seaport on Burrard Inlet, whose harbor stays free of ice throughout the year. The metropolitan area has a population of about 1,380,000.

The Northwest Indians
Carved totem poles are a reminder of the rich cultural traditions of the Indian peoples of the Pacific northwest. The poles were placed outside the wooden houses of important families to show their ancestry.

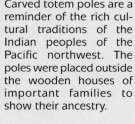

Stikine

Coast

B R I

Skeena

M o u n t a i n s

C O L U

Prince Rupert

Queen Charlotte Islands

Mt. Waddington
13,261

Vancouver Island

| 0 | 100 | 200 | 300 Km |

| 0 | | 100 | 200 Miles |

Victoria

Logging in British Columbia

A powerful truck hauls lumber along a forest trail in the province of British Columbia. Over half of Canada's great forests are harvested. The wood is now usually hauled to sawmills. A large amount is pulped and made into paper. The hard life of the lumberjacks is a part of Canadian tradition. Their job has been made easier by new equipment.

Grain elevators in Alberta

Storage elevators line the railroad tracks at Innisfail, in Alberta. Harvested grain is taken by rail to cities and ports. The Canadian prairies are one of the world's most important wheat-growing areas, and the provinces of Saskatchewan, Alberta and Manitoba are major producers. The Canadian prairies have long, bitter winters, but hardy types of wheat have been bred which ripen quickly. They can be sown when the snow melts in late spring and are harvested by August. Other hardy crops include oats, barley, rye, and rapeseed. Prairie farms are large and mechanized. Huge combine-harvesters make short work of large fields.

UNITED STATES OF AMERICA

The United States of America is the fourth largest country in the world. It is made up of 50 states, 48 of which lie between Canada and Mexico. The other two are the islands of Hawaii in the Pacific Ocean, and Alaska in the north-western corner of North America, which was bought from the Russians in 1867.

The U.S.A. is a country of great natural resources. Between the Rocky Mountains in the west and the Appalachian Mountains in the east lie huge areas of prairie land where corn, wheat, soybeans, and many other crops are grown on highly mechanized farms. Despite large reserves of oil in Alaska, the U.S.A. is such a huge consumer that it still has to import stocks of oil.

cont. page 34

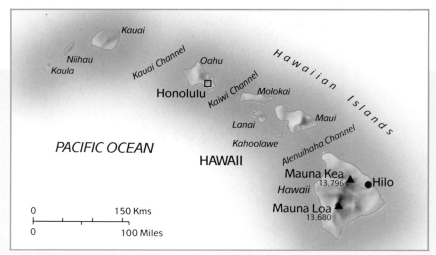

Kauai

Niihau
Kaula

Kauai Channel

Kauai Channel

Oahu

Honolulu

Kaiwi Channel

Molokai

Hawaiian Islands

Lanai

Maui

Kahoolawe

Alenuihaha Channel

PACIFIC OCEAN

HAWAII

Mauna Kea
13,796

Hilo

Hawaii

Mauna Loa
13,680

0   150 Kms

0   100 Miles

C. Flattery

Seattle
Olympia
Mt. Rainier WASHINGTON
14,409
Portland
Salem

Great Falls
Helena

Coast Range

Cascade Range

O R E G O N

Snake

M O N

Boise
I D A H O

Yello
Natio

RO

Sacramento

Carson City

Oakland

San Francisco

Great
Basin

Great
Salt
Lake

Salt Lake
City

NEVADA

UTAH

C A L I F O R N I A

Sierra Nevada

Mt Whitney
14,494

Las Vegas

Grand
Canyon

Colorado

Coast Range

Los Angeles
Long Beach

San Diego

A R I Z O N A

Phoenix

Gila

Tucson

Bryce Canyon, Utah

Bryce Canyon is about 90 miles north of the Grand Canyon. Centuries of erosion from wind and frost have produced this spectacle of brilliantly colored spires. The canyon is a large U-shaped amphitheater, one mile wide.

Wildlife in the U.S.A.

Three animals from the great variety of wildlife in the U.S.A.
1. CALIFORNIA SEALION
2. RACCOON
3. BALD EAGLE

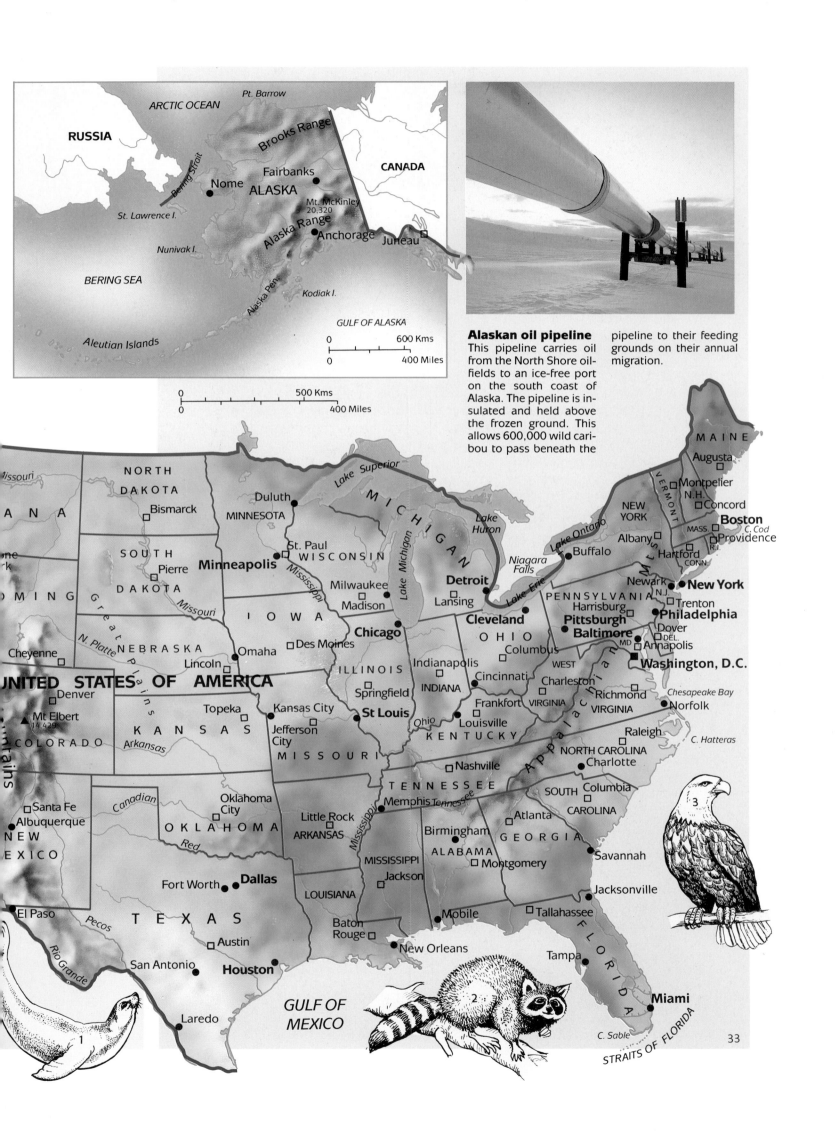

ARCTIC OCEAN
Pt. Barrow

RUSSIA

Brooks Range

CANADA

Nome
Fairbanks
ALASKA
Mt. McKinley
20,320
Bering Strait
St. Lawrence I.
Alaska Range
Anchorage
Juneau

Nunivak I.

BERING SEA

Alaska Pen.

Kodiak I.

GULF OF ALASKA

Aleutian Islands

0   600 Kms
0   400 Miles

Alaskan oil pipeline
This pipeline carries oil
from the North Shore oil-
fields to an ice-free port
on the south coast of
Alaska. The pipeline is in-
sulated and held above
the frozen ground. This
allows 600,000 wild cari-
bou to pass beneath the

pipeline to their feeding
grounds on their annual
migration.

0   500 Kms
0   400 Miles

Missouri

NORTH
DAKOTA

Lake Superior

MICHIGAN

MAINE
Augusta

Duluth
Bismarck
MINNESOTA

Lake
Huron

VERMONT
Montpelier
N.H.
Concord
NEW
YORK
Boston
C. Cod

St. Paul
WISCONSIN
Minneapolis

SOUTH
DAKOTA
Pierre

Milwaukee
Madison

Lake Michigan

Lansing

Lake Ontario
Niagara
Falls
Buffalo
Lake Erie

Albany
MASS.
Providence
R.I.
Hartford
CONN

Detroit

Cleveland

PENNSYLVANIA
Harrisburg

Newark
N.J.
New York
Trenton
Philadelphia

IOWA

Chicago

OHIO
Columbus

Pittsburgh
Baltimore
MD
Dover
DEL.
Annapolis

Mississippi
Missouri

WYOMING
Great Plains

NEBRASKA
Cheyenne
N. Platte

Des Moines

Omaha
Lincoln

ILLINOIS

Indianapolis

Cincinnati

WEST
VIRGINIA
Charleston

Washington, D.C.

Richmond
VIRGINIA

Chesapeake Bay

Norfolk

UNITED STATES OF AMERICA
Denver

Topeka
Kansas City

INDIANA
Springfield

St Louis

Ohio
Frankfort

Louisville

KENTUCKY

Raleigh

C. Hatteras

Mt Elbert
14,429
COLORADO
Arkansas

KANSAS
Jefferson
City

MISSOURI

Nashville

Tennessee

NORTH CAROLINA
Charlotte

Santa Fe
Albuquerque
NEW
MEXICO

Canadian

Oklahoma
City

OKLAHOMA
Red

Little Rock
ARKANSAS

Mississippi

Memphis
Tennessee

Birmingham

ALABAMA
Montgomery

GEORGIA

SOUTH
CAROLINA
Columbia

Atlanta

Savannah

El Paso
Pecos

Fort Worth
Dallas

TEXAS

MISSISSIPPI
Jackson

LOUISIANA

Mobile

Tallahassee

Jacksonville

FLORIDA

Rio Grande

Austin
San Antonio
Houston

Baton
Rouge
New Orleans

GULF OF
MEXICO

Tampa

C. Sable

Miami

STRAITS OF FLORIDA

Laredo

33

Heavy industry is concentrated in the northeast and around the Great Lakes, but more recently high-tech and light industries have developed in the west, especially in California, which is now the biggest manufacturing state in the U.S.

People have come from every continent to live in the U.S. The early European settlers learned much about their new home from the American Indians. While most immigrants came in search of a better life, black people were brought over by force from West Africa to work as slaves on Southern plantations. Huge numbers of European immigrants arrived in the late nineteenth century, followed by waves of newcomers from Asia and Latin America in this century.

The U.S. is famous for many things: its space technology which put the first man on the Moon; New York City with its skyscrapers and important financial center; the film industry in Hollywood; and its beautiful national parks such as the Grand Canyon and Yellowstone.

Navajo Indians
Many Indians live in areas set aside for them called reservations. The Navajo reservation in the southwest is the largest.

Farming in southern California
These men are loading lettuce onto a truck. California, on the west coast of the U.S.A., sells more farm products than any other state. Particular areas of California specialize in particular crops – citrus fruits and grapes are cultivated in central California.

Pittsburgh (top)
Pittsburgh is one of the major centers of heavy manufacturing in the northern U.S.A. with large iron and steel and chemical works.

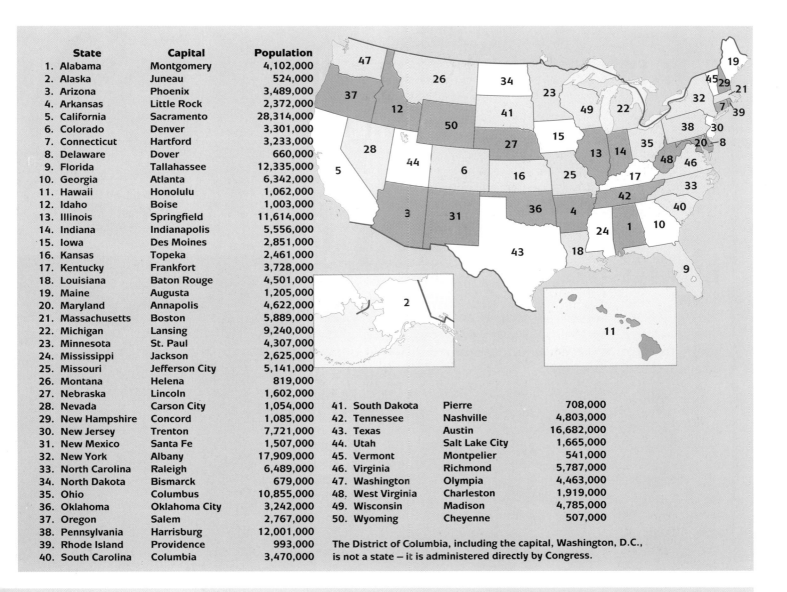

State	Capital	Population
1. Alabama	Montgomery	4,102,000
2. Alaska	Juneau	524,000
3. Arizona	Phoenix	3,489,000
4. Arkansas	Little Rock	2,372,000
5. California	Sacramento	28,314,000
6. Colorado	Denver	3,301,000
7. Connecticut	Hartford	3,233,000
8. Delaware	Dover	660,000
9. Florida	Tallahassee	12,335,000
10. Georgia	Atlanta	6,342,000
11. Hawaii	Honolulu	1,062,000
12. Idaho	Boise	1,003,000
13. Illinois	Springfield	11,614,000
14. Indiana	Indianapolis	5,556,000
15. Iowa	Des Moines	2,851,000
16. Kansas	Topeka	2,461,000
17. Kentucky	Frankfort	3,728,000
18. Louisiana	Baton Rouge	4,501,000
19. Maine	Augusta	1,205,000
20. Maryland	Annapolis	4,622,000
21. Massachusetts	Boston	5,889,000
22. Michigan	Lansing	9,240,000
23. Minnesota	St. Paul	4,307,000
24. Mississippi	Jackson	2,625,000
25. Missouri	Jefferson City	5,141,000
26. Montana	Helena	819,000
27. Nebraska	Lincoln	1,602,000
28. Nevada	Carson City	1,054,000
29. New Hampshire	Concord	1,085,000
30. New Jersey	Trenton	7,721,000
31. New Mexico	Santa Fe	1,507,000
32. New York	Albany	17,909,000
33. North Carolina	Raleigh	6,489,000
34. North Dakota	Bismarck	679,000
35. Ohio	Columbus	10,855,000
36. Oklahoma	Oklahoma City	3,242,000
37. Oregon	Salem	2,767,000
38. Pennsylvania	Harrisburg	12,001,000
39. Rhode Island	Providence	993,000
40. South Carolina	Columbia	3,470,000
41. South Dakota	Pierre	708,000
42. Tennessee	Nashville	4,803,000
43. Texas	Austin	16,682,000
44. Utah	Salt Lake City	1,665,000
45. Vermont	Montpelier	541,000
46. Virginia	Richmond	5,787,000
47. Washington	Olympia	4,463,000
48. West Virginia	Charleston	1,919,000
49. Wisconsin	Madison	4,785,000
50. Wyoming	Cheyenne	507,000

The District of Columbia, including the capital, Washington, D.C., is not a state — it is administered directly by Congress.

Jazz band, New Orleans

The first jazz bands started in the city of New Orleans in the South. The "Great Age" of jazz was in the 1920s when New Orleans was a colorful and cosmopolitan city. Groups of black musicians would play together spontaneously and new styles of dancing developed. Much of today's pop music originated from jazz.

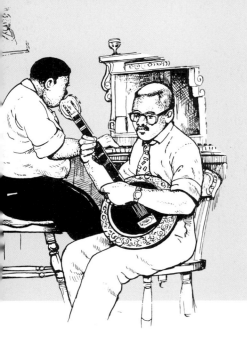

New Hampshire in the fall

The far northeastern corner of the U.S., known as New England, is renowned for the colors of the leaves in the fall. Outdoor sports such as fishing, hunting, and skiing are very popular in the unspoilt countryside. This is the land that the Pilgrims from Britain settled in the early seventeenth century, and many of the place names are derived from towns and villages in England.

NORTHEASTERN U.S.

If you take a plane by night along the northeastern seaboard of the United States, you will see the black expanse of the Atlantic Ocean fringed by a vast, glittering array of lights. These belong to some of America's greatest cities, including New York City, the largest of all, with a population of over seven million. The northeastern states are the most densely populated in the country.

The mild climate of the northeast region, and its position on Atlantic trading routes, attracted large numbers of European settlers to the region from the seventeenth century onwards. The forests were stripped, and within 200 years were replaced by mines and factories. Coal, iron and steel created sprawling industrial cities such as Pittsburgh. The region still contains some of America's finest natural landscapes, from the rocky shores of New England to the Adirondack mountains and the mighty Niagara Falls.

Industry in the northeast
Steel being processed and machined at a mill. Pennsylvania alone can produce over 12 million' tons of steel in a year, helping to make the U.S. the world's third largest producer, after the Soviet Union and Japan. The northeastern states are a center for traditional industries such as chemicals, machinery manufacture, food processing, and printing. Forestry, farming and fishing are an important part of the economy in New England.

Amish farmers
The state of Pennsylvania was founded in 1681 by an English Quaker, William Penn, as a refuge for fellow Quakers and others seeking to escape religious persecution. Later immigrants included German speakers, known as Pennsylvania Dutch (from *deutsch,* meaning "German"). Amongst these were the Amish and the Mennonites, members of conservative Protestant sects. Their communities *(above)* have survived in several parts of North America. They still use horse-drawn plows and carts and wear simple, homemade clothes.

New York in winter

New York City is the largest urban center in the U.S., and one of the most famous cities in the world. The city was founded by Dutch settlers and called New Amsterdam, but was renamed by the British, who ruled it until independence.

During the nineteenth century countless immigrants arrived in the city from Europe, dreaming of wealth and freedom. The buildings which soon made up the city skyline reflected this dream. The center of the city was the island of Manhattan, bounded by the Hudson and the East Rivers. Here there was little room for buildings to spread outwards, and so, after the invention of the passenger elevator, skyscrapers were built. The Empire State Building, opened in 1931, is 1250 feet high, or 1414 feet including the mast on the top. The World Trade Center, completed in 1973, is 1350 feet tall.

Manhattan remains the center of New York City. Its streets are household names around the world: Wall Street, Broadway, Fifth Avenue. Here are found the headquarters of the United Nations, St. Patrick's Cathedral, famous theaters, and art galleries. The city is renowned for its pace and energy, but Central Park *(above)* offers respite from the traffic and crowds. The city has now spread far beyond Manhattan, to include the Bronx, Queens, and Brooklyn.

Mark Twain's house

The house of one of America's best-loved writers is in Hartford, Connecticut. Samuel Langhorne Clemens (1835-1910) under the name "Mark Twain" wrote *Tom Sawyer* (1876) and *Huckleberry Finn* (1884).

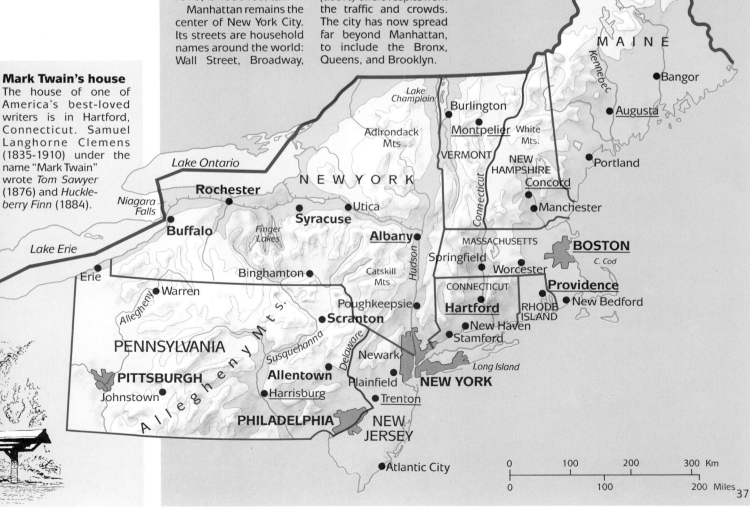

MAINE

Bangor

Augusta

Lake Champlain

Burlington

Montpelier   White Mts.

Adirondack Mts.

VERMONT   NEW HAMPSHIRE

Kennebec

Portland

Concord

Lake Ontario

NEW YORK

Manchester

Rochester

Utica

Niagara Falls

Syracuse

Finger Lakes

Buffalo

Albany

MASSACHUSETTS

Springfield

BOSTON

C. Cod

Lake Erie

Binghamton

Catskill Mts

Worcester

Providence

Erie

Warren

CONNECTICUT

Hudson

Connecticut

New Bedford

Allegheny

Poughkeepsie

Hartford

RHODE ISLAND

PENNSYLVANIA

Scranton

New Haven

Stamford

Susquehanna

Delaware

Newark

Long Island

PITTSBURGH

Allentown

Plainfield

NEW YORK

Johnstown

Harrisburg

Trenton

PHILADELPHIA   NEW JERSEY

Atlantic City

Allegheny Mts.

| 0 | 100 | 200 | 300 Km |
| 0 | 100 | 200 Miles |

CENTRAL U.S.

The region to the west of the Ohio River and north of the Ozark plateaus is traditionally known as the Midwest. The eastern part of the region was one of the first areas of the United States to become heavily industrialized, with coal mines and factories. To the north, the Great Lakes form the border with Canada. Here too are major manufacturing cities and centers of commerce, such as Milwaukee, Chicago, and Detroit. The western part of the region is mainly agricultural. Crops include cereals such as wheat, corn and oats, roots such as potatoes and beets, and soybeans.

Much of the farmland was once open prairie, grassland roamed by herds of bison. These were hunted by the Indians of the Plains. As white settlers traveled westwards in the last century, they siezed Indian lands, built towns and railroads, and slaughtered the bison in their millions, most often for sport.

The Badlands
The prairies of South Dakota are broken above the White River by a bleak region of rocks and stone. Although this area has its own strange beauty, the land is barren. It was of little use to the Plains Indians, to the first French trappers, or to pioneers from back east, and so became known as the "Badlands."

Agriculture in the Midwest
The region between the Appalachians and the Rockies is fertile and mostly well watered. Over 95 percent of Iowa is farmed, making it the richest state in the agricultural Midwest. Nebraska and Kansas, too, are farming states and major wheat producers. Cattle and hogs are also raised on midwestern farms, with Wisconsin the leading producer of dairy products.

The Gateway Arch
The Gateway Arch in St. Louis, Missouri, symbolizing the gateway to the West, is the tallest monument in the U.S. Capsule trains and stairs lead to a viewing room 630 feet above the ground.

The "Windy City"
Bridges are raised to allow boats to pass on the Chicago river, beneath Chicago's city skyline. Once famed for its stock-yards and its gangsters, Chicago is today the third largest city in the U.S. with a population of over three million. It is a center of manufacture and commerce, and boasts the world's highest sky-scraper. The Sears Tower has 110 stories and is 1454 feet high. The strong, cold wind off Lake Michigan, called "the hawk" by natives, gave Chicago its nickname, the "Windy City."

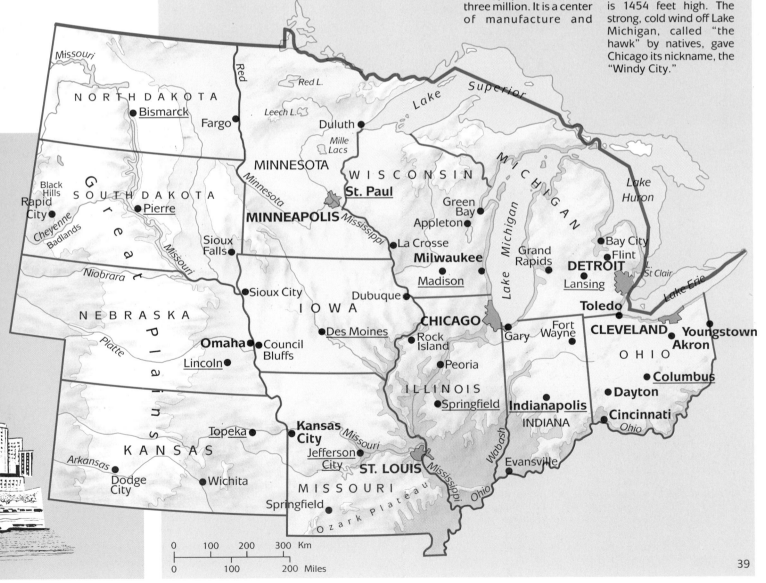

Missouri

NORTH DAKOTA
Bismarck
Fargo

Red
Red L.
Leech L.

Duluth
Mille Lacs

MINNESOTA

Black Hills
Rapid City
Cheyenne
Badlands

SOUTH DAKOTA
Pierre

Great

WISCONSIN
St. Paul
MINNEAPOLIS

Green Bay
Appleton

MICHIGAN

Lake Superior
Lake Huron

Niobrara

Missouri

Sioux Falls

Minnesota

Mississippi

La Crosse
Milwaukee
Madison

Lake Michigan

Grand Rapids

Bay City
Flint
DETROIT

L. St Clair

Lansing

NEBRASKA

P l a i n s

Sioux City

IOWA
Des Moines

Dubuque

CHICAGO
Rock Island

Gary

Fort Wayne

Lake Erie

Toledo

CLEVELAND
Youngstown
Akron

OHIO

Platte

Omaha
Council Bluffs

Lincoln

Peoria

ILLINOIS
Springfield

Indianapolis
INDIANA

Columbus
Dayton
Cincinnati
Ohio

Topeka

Kansas City
Missouri

K A N S A S

Arkansas
Dodge City
Wichita

Jefferson City
ST. LOUIS
MISSOURI
Springfield

Mississippi

Wabash

Evansville

Ohio

Ozark Plateau

0   100   200   300 Km
0   100   200 Miles

SOUTHERN U.S.

The wooded ridges of the Appalachian mountains run southwards from Canada through Virginia and the Carolinas. Florida stretches into the Gulf of Mexico and has more coastline than any other state except Alaska. It attracts many tourists every year with its warm climate and beautiful beaches. Swamps and bayous fringe the other states which border the Gulf. Farther west, Texas is the second largest state; its 262,017 square miles support extensive farms, cattle ranches, and oil production facilities.

The great Mississippi River links Louisiana and the southern states with St. Louis in the north. In its valley advanced Indian cultures developed in the eighth century AD. From the sixteenth century onwards, the southeast was colonized by the Spanish, English and French. Their plantations, growing cotton and tobacco, employed slaves brought from Africa. One result of the Civil War of 1861-65 was the freeing of the slaves.

Johnson Space Center, Houston
A colossal Saturn V rocket, 365 feet long, on show at the Johnson Space Center in Houston, Texas. Rockets like this one pioneered space travel; they were used in the

Apollo missions to the Moon in the 1960s and 70s. In Florida, the John F. Kennedy Space Center at Cape Canaveral has been the chief launching site for the United States space program since 1977.

A Mississippi river trip
Once these Mississippi riverboats carried gamblers and gunfighters upstream from New Orleans. Today, they carry tourists.

Washington, D.C.

In 1790, Congress authorized the building of a federal capital designed by the French architect Pierre Charles L'Enfant. Its site was to be on the Potomac River, on territory acquired from the states of Maryland and Virginia.

The District of Columbia (D.C.) today occupies about 69 square miles. The district is not part of any state, and its land is owned by the government. Washington, D.C. is one of the world's most impressive capital cities, with broad grassy avenues and memorials to great Americans, including George Washington (1732-99), Thomas Jefferson (1743-1826) and Abraham Lincoln (1809-65). At the bottom of the Mall is the magnificent dome of the Capitol *(left).* begun in 1793. This is the center of government, the scene of debates in the Senate and the House of Representatives. On the northern side of the Mall is the White House, the official residence of the U.S. President. Originally built between 1792 and 1800, much of it was burned down during a British attack in 1814, but was restored and extended in later years.

Fall in Virginia

The Blue Ridge Parkway runs for 469 miles through the states of Virginia and North Carolina towards Tennessee. It follows the rolling Appalachian ranges, and passes through beautiful forests whose leaves turn to every shade of brown, red, yellow, and gold in the Fall. Maple, oak, hickory, and birch are found amongst spruce and pine.

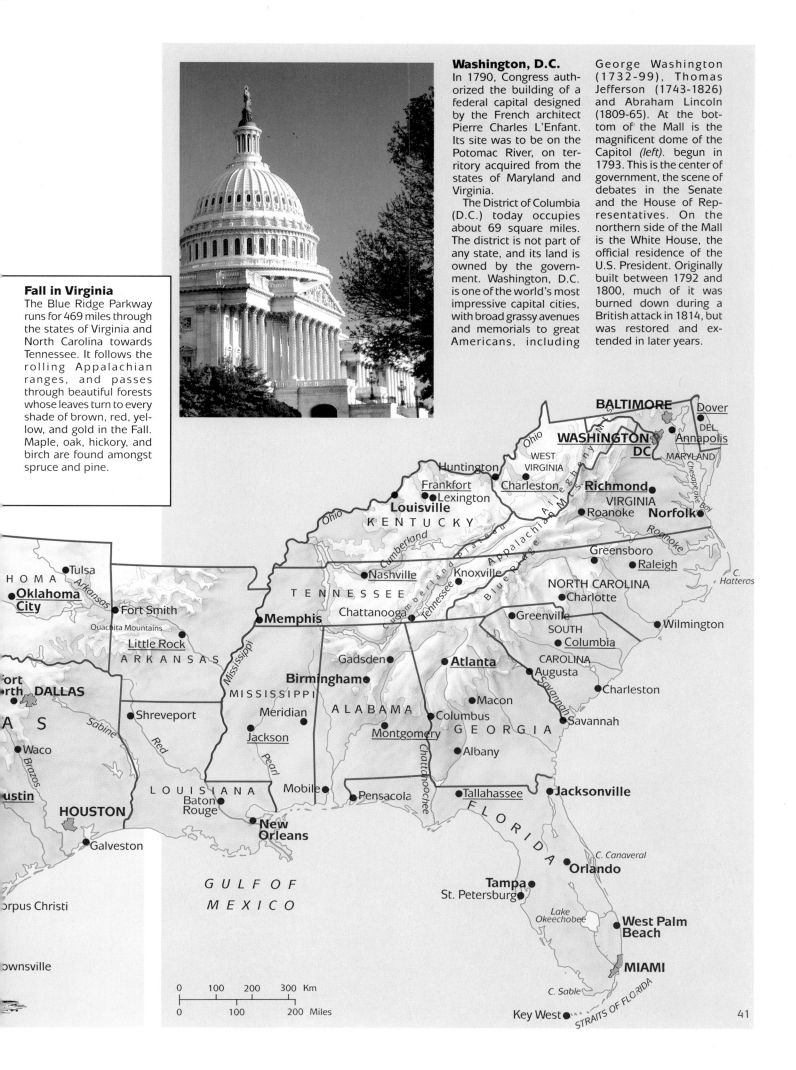

41

WESTERN U.S.

When the nineteenth-century pioneers traveled westwards in search of a new home, they faced all kinds of hardship. The western landscape still presents a challenge today. The massive ranges of the Rocky Mountains run southwards from Canada, and beyond lie the deserts, salt flats, and canyons of Utah and Nevada. The southwestern states of New Mexico and Arizona are also lands of burning sand and barren rock. Before the Pacific Ocean is reached, more mountain chains must be crossed – the Sierra Nevada in the south and the Cascade ranges in the north.

The West Coast was no disappointment to those early pioneers and has continued to fascinate Americans from other regions. The northwestern states of Washington and Oregon are cool and heavily forested. Farther south, modern California has an economy larger than that of most independent nations, and Los Angeles has long been known for its movies and its recording industry. The state is now also world-famous as a center of computer technology.

Beautiful San Francisco
The Golden Gate Bridge spans the strait linking San Francisco Bay to the Pacific Ocean. With its mild, spring-like climate, and its spectacular views over the Pacific Ocean, San Francisco is one of the most beautiful cities in North America. Its buildings range from ornate wooden houses built in the last century on the city's steep hillsides, to the gleaming offices of the downtown area.

The salty lake
California's Mono Lake lies near the Sierra Nevada, and its salty waters are full of strange, tall white towers of the porous rock known as tufa. Formed out of calcium carbonate, many of these towers have been revealed as the water level of the lake has dropped over the years through evaporation.

Frontier town
Cody, Wyoming, named for "Buffalo" Bill Cody, brings back memories of the days when the West was wild frontier territory.

Chaco Canyon

Hundreds of years ago, Chaco Canyon in New Mexico was home to the Anasazi Indians. It contained an extensive road network. The Pueblo Bonito site housed about a thousand people. They hunted, grew crops, made pottery, and traded with people far away to the south. Chaco Canyon flourished from about A.D. 950 to 1300, when the dwellings were mysteriously abandoned.

C. Flattery

WASHINGTON

Seattle
Tacoma
Olympia ▲Mt. Rainier
14,409

Spokane

Great Falls

MONTANA

Missouri

Yellowstone

Helena
Butte

Billings

Portland
Salem

Columbia

Blue
Mts.

OREGON

Eugene

IDAHO

Rocky

Yellowstone
National Park

WYOMING

Boise

Snake

Pocatello

Casper

North
Platte

Mendocino

Great
Humboldt

Great
Salt
Lake

Ogden

Cheyenne

South Platte

Salt Lake City

NEVADA

Provo

Denver

Reno

Carson City

UTAH

Mt. Elbert
▲14,429

Colorado Springs

Sacramento

Basin

Wasatch Range

Colorado

Pueblo

Arkansas

Oakland

Yosemite
National Park

COLORADO

SAN
FRANCISCO

CALIFORNIA

Sierra

Bryce
Canyon

Lake
Powell

Fresno

Nevada

▲Mt. Whitney
14,494

Las Vegas

Death
Valley

Lake
Mead

Grand
Canyon

Painted
Desert

Santa Fe

Bakersfield

Coast

Range

Mojave
Desert

Flagstaff

Albuquerque

Santa Barbara

San Bernardino

ARIZONA

NEW MEXICO

LOS ANGELES
Long
Beach

Salton
Sea

Roswell

Colorado

Phoenix

SAN DIEGO

Gila

Rio Grande

Pecos

Tucson

0   100   200   300 Km

0   100   200 Miles

43

CENTRAL AMERICA AND MEXICO

Mexico and the Central American countries — Guatemala, Nicaragua, El Salvador, Honduras, Belize, Costa Rica, and Panama — form a long land bridge joining North and South America. Mexico is the largest of these countries — in fact more people live in its capital, Mexico City, than in any of the Central American states.

The people of Mexico and Central America are descended from the original Indian tribes that inhabited the area, and from the Spanish who arrived in the sixteenth century. Many people are of mixed Indian and Spanish blood and are known as *mestizos*.

Mexico has valuable natural reserves of gold and silver, and large oil fields in the Gulf of Mexico. The economies of the Central American countries rely heavily on the export of crops such as cotton, bananas, and sugar.

A market in Xochimilco, Mexico
This woman is weaving a traditional rug at a market. Handweaving is an ancient Indian art that is still practiced, especially in the south where there is a larger native Indian population. Styles vary according to region so that the region which an Indian comes from can be identified by the colors and patterns on their clothes and rugs.

Cacti in the Mexican desert

The cactus plant is often the only form of life in the deserts of northern Mexico. Some years there is no rain at all, especially in Lower California. However, there are hundreds of different species of cacti, and some yield juices which are turned into alcoholic drinks. One of these is called *tequila*, and is used to make cocktails. Plantations are now run to produce tequila for export, as it has become popular around the world. A stronger and cheaper drink, which has been made since the days of the Mayans, is *pulque*, known as the poor Mexican's beer. The juice is squeezed from the fleshy leaves of a very tall variety of cactus, often taller than a person.

The Panama Canal

The Panama Canal is one of the greatest feats of engineering in the world. It is 40 miles long, and was built so that ships could pass between the Atlantic and Pacific Oceans without having to sail south around South America. This involved hacking out miles of rock, damming rivers and building huge iron locks. It was completed by the U.S.A. but is now jointly administered by the U.S.A. and Panama. The canal is very important to world trade and shipping companies have to pay a high toll to the Panamanian government for its use. The canal brings many jobs for the local people.

Cutting bananas
The banana is one of the most important crops grown in the countries of Central America. Machetes are used to cut the clumps of bananas while they are still green. They are then exported to the U.S.A. and Europe in time for them to ripen just before delivery to the shops.

uahua
Rio Grande
Nuevo Laredo
Sierra Madre Oriental
ICO
Torreón
Saltillo
Matamoros
Monterrey
San Luis Potosí
Tampico
Aguascalientes
León
Querétaro
dalajara
Grande de Santiago
Morelia
Mexico City
Veracruz
Cuernavaca
Citlaltepetl
18,700
Puebla
Balsas
Orizaba
Acapulco
Oaxaca
Minatitlán
Isthmus of Tehuantepec

GULF OF MEXICO

I. de Cozumel
Mérida
Gulf of Campeche
Yucatán
Belmopan
Belize City
BELIZE

Gulf of Tehuantepec
GUATEMALA
Guatemala City
HONDURAS
Tegucigalpa
San Salvador
EL SALVADOR
NICARAGUA
Managua
L. Nicaragua
C. Gracias á Dios
Mosquito Coast

PACIFIC OCEAN

COSTA RICA
San José
Panama Canal
Panama
PANAMA
Gulf of Panama

0   500 Km
0   400 Miles

CARIBBEAN ISLANDS

The islands of the West Indies lie between North and South America. Commonly known as the Caribbean, this region contains 24 countries whose populations range in size from a few thousand to over 10 million, and whose people speak five main languages as well as many other local dialects.

Today over half of the countries of the Caribbean are politically independent; others, such as the British Virgin Islands and Guadeloupe, are still colonies. The wealth of the Caribbean countries varies immensely. Puerto Rico has a well-developed industrial base. Many of the islands have thriving tourist industries. In contrast, Haiti is one of the poorest countries in the western hemisphere.

The tropical climate of this region is especially suited to growing sugarcane, which is used to produce sugar, molasses (a kind of syrup), and rum for export. Other crops include coffee, tobacco, cacao (to make chocolate and cocoa), and citrus fruits.

GULF OF MEXICO

Straits of Florida

■ **Havana**

Santa Clara

Cienfu

I. de Juventud

Grand Cayman (Br.)

Cayman Is. (Br.)

Cutting sugarcane in Cuba

Sugarcane is Cuba's most valuable crop. It makes up 80 percent of its exports. Long machetes are used to cut down the cane, which is then taken to the sugar mills for processing. The cane is ground in the mill and boiled in water until sugar crystals are formed. Cuba is one of the top three sugar producers in the world.

Festival time

Music can be heard everywhere at carnival time in the Caribbean. People dress in traditional costumes and dance in the streets. Reggae music from Jamaica and calypso songs from Trinidad are especially popular. The musical instruments include drums from hollow logs, and shakers from dried gourds.

46

Curaçao

Many of the Caribbean islands show the influence of the European settlers in the past. Curaçao was first occupied by the Spanish and then by the Dutch. Many of its buildings today — churches, halls, schools, and houses — were erected by the colonists. The main language spoken on Curaçao is Dutch. Also spoken is a patois that developed from the earliest contacts between Europeans and Africans who were brought to the island as slaves.

Bartering for fish

Fish is often sold straight from the boat in the Caribbean. Local fishers sail along the busy quayside, where in some places there are floating markets. Everybody gathers round to see the fresh catch and the bartering begins. The people shout out offers for particular pieces of fish, depending on the type and size. There is a rich diversity of fish in the Caribbean Sea and it is an important food of the islands.

Hamilton
Bermuda (Br.)

Gt. Abaco I.
ma I.

New Providence I.
Eleuthera I.
Nassau
BAHAMAS
Andros I.
Cat. I.

Long I.

CUBA

Camagüey
Acklins I.
Caicos Is. (Br.)
Holguín
Gt. Inagua I.
Turks Is. (Br.)
Guantánamo
Santiago de Cuba

Windward Passage

Santiago
HAITI
Port-au-Prince
DOMINICAN REPUBLIC
Santo Domingo

Mona Passage

San Juan
Virgin Is. (U.S.)
Virgin Is. (Br.)
Leeward Islands
Anguilla (Br.)
St. Martin (Fr./Neth.)
Neth. Antilles
ANTIGUA AND BARBUDA
ST. KITTS – NEVIS

AMAICA **Kingston**

A n t i l l e s

Hispaniola
Ponce
Puerto Rico (U.S.)
St Croix

Montserrat (Br.)
Guadeloupe (Fr.)
Basse-Terre

CARIBBEAN

SEA

Lesser Antilles
Roseau **DOMINICA**

Martinique (Fr.)
Fort-de-France

Windward Islands

ST. LUCIA
ST. VINCENT AND THE GRENADINES
BARBADOS

0   300 Km
0   200 Miles

Aruba
Netherlands Antilles
Curaçao
Bonaire
GRENADA

Willemstad

Tobago

Port of Spain
TRINIDAD AND TOBAGO
Trinidad

47

SOUTH AMERICA

S outh America stretches from the Caribbean Sea, well above the Equator, down to Cape Horn, the cold southernmost tip which is only 615 miles away from Antarctica. It is made up of 13 countries; the largest is Brazil which covers nearly half of the total area of the continent.

The Andes mountains run almost the entire length of South America, with peaks up to 23,000 feet. Spanning the continent, from its source in the Peruvian Andes through the Brazilian rainforest to the Atlantic Ocean, is the mighty Amazon river, at 4050 miles the second longest river in the world. South of the rainforest are the plateau grasslands of the Pampas. To the west of the Andes, squeezed between the coast and the mountains, lies the Atacama Desert, reputedly the driest desert in the world.

The Straits of Magellan in southern Chile.

South America:

Highest point Mount Aconcagua (Argentina) 22,834ft. (6960m.) above sea level
Lowest point Peninsula Valdés (Argentina) 131ft. (40m.) below sea level

Longest river Amazon 4050mi. (6515km.)
Largest lake Titicaca (Peru/Bolivia) 3220 sq.mi. (8340 sq.km.)

ARGENTINA
Official name República Argentina
Area 1,068,302 sq. miles (2,766,889 sq. km.)
Population 32,300,000
Capital Buenos Aires (pop. 2,922,829)
Largest cities Córdoba (982,018)
Rosario (954,606)
Mendoza (596,796)
La Plata (560,341)
Tucumán (496,914)
Mar del Plata (407,024)
Currency Austral
Official language(s) Spanish
Chief products Meat products (especially beef and mutton), wool, oil, minerals (coal, lead, zinc, and iron ore), natural gas, wine, machine tools, vehicles, textiles, wheat, corn
Exports Meat, cereals, wool
Imports Machinery, iron and steel, nonferrous metals

BRAZIL
Official name República Federativa do Brasil
Area 3,286,488 sq. miles (8,511,965 sq. km.)
Population 150,400,000
Capital Brasília (pop. 1,567,709)
Largest cities São Paulo (10,063,110)
Rio de Janeiro (5,603,388)
Belo Horizonte (2,114,429)
Salvador (1,804,438)
Fortaleza (1,582,414)
Nova Iguaçu (1,319,491)
Currency New Cruzado
Official language(s) Portuguese (Italian, Spanish, German, Japanese, Arabic are also spoken)
Chief products Iron ore, manganese, bauxite, chrome, diamonds, corn, black beans, cassava, coffee, cotton, soy, rice
Exports Coffee, cotton, iron ore, machinery
Imports Machinery, crude oil, cereals, nonferrous metals

BOLIVIA
Official name República de Bolivia
Area 424,164 sq. miles (1,098,581 sq. km.)
Population 7,300,000
Capital La Paz (Legal capital – Sucre)
Official language(s) Spanish
Chief products Tin, natural gas, coffee, wood, natural rubber, potatoes, corn

CHILE
Official name República de Chile
Area 292,132 sq. miles (756,626 sq. km.)
Population 13,200,000
Capital Santiago
Official language(s) Spanish
Chief products Copper, nitrate, wheat, livestock, fish, iron ore, lumber, vegetables, fruit, silver

COLOMBIA
Official name República de Colombia
Area 440,831 sq. miles (1,141,748 sq. km.)
Population 31,800,000
Capital Bogotá
Official language(s) Spanish
Chief products Coffee, cotton, bananas, tobacco, gold, coal, oil, textiles, precious stones

ECUADOR
Official name República del Ecuador
Area 178,130 sq. miles (461,475 sq. km.)
Population 10,700,000
Capital Quito
Official language(s) Spanish
Chief products Bananas, coffee, cocoa, oil, rice, fish (especially shrimps and sardines), African palm

PERU
Official name República del Perú
Area 496,225 sq. miles (1,285,216 sq. km.)
Population 21,900,000
Capital Lima (pop. 5,008,400)
Largest cities Arequipa (561,338)
Iquitos (540,560)
Chiclayo (533,266)
Currency Inti
Official language(s) Spanish and Quechua
Chief products Fishmeal, iron ore, copper, silver, zinc, lead, sugar, wheat, corn, oil, lumber, cotton

VENEZUELA
Official name República de Venezuela
Area 352,144 sq. miles (912,050 sq. km.)
Population 19,600,000
Capital Caracas
Official language(s) Spanish
Chief products Oil, petrochemicals, aluminum, plastics, steel products, gold, diamonds, asbestos, textiles

GUYANA
Official name The Co-operative Republic of Guyana
Area 83,000 sq. miles (214,969 sq. km.)
Population 971,000
Capital Georgetown
Official language(s) English
Chief products Sugar, rice, bauxite, alumina, diamonds, gold, lumber, rum

Beautiful scenery high in the Andes.

PARAGUAY
Official name República del Paraguay
Area 157,042 sq. miles (406,752 sq. km.)
Population 4,300,000
Capital Asunción
Official language(s) Spanish (Guarini is also spoken)
Chief products Processed meat, cotton, soya beans, tobacco, sugar, coffee, lumber

URUGUAY
Official name República Oriental del Uruguay
Area 68,037 sq. miles (176,215 sq. km.)
Population 3,058,000
Capital Montevideo
Official language(s) Spanish
Chief products Wool, meat products, textiles, fish, fruits, wheat, barley, corn, oil products

SURINAME
Official name Nieuwe Republiek van Suriname
Area 63,037 sq. miles (163,265 sq. km.)
Population 394,768
Capital Paramaribo
Official language(s) Dutch, English
Chief products Lumber, rice, sugarcane, bauxite

FALKLAND ISLANDS (U.K.)
Area 4700 sq. miles (12,175 sq. km.)
Population 1919
Capital Port Stanley

FRENCH GUIANA
Official name Guyane Française
Area 34,750 sq. miles (90,000 sq. km.)
Population 84,180
Capital Cayenne
Official language(s) French (Creole is also spoken)
Chief products Fish (especially shrimps), lumber, cayenne pepper

NORTHERN SOUTH AMERICA

The landscape of the countries of this region varies from the mountain ranges and plains of the Andes mountains in the west to the tropical rainforests of the north.

Many of the countries have rich mineral resources. Venezuela is a leading producer of oil, Colombia mines emeralds, gold, and coal; silver, zinc, iron, and tin have all been discovered in the mountainous areas of Bolivia and Pèru. Agriculture varies from the subsistence farming practiced by the Bolivian Indians on the high plateau around Lake Titicaca to the high levels of production of a country such as Ecuador, which is a leading exporter of bananas.

The people of these countries are descended from the native Indians and the European settlers who conquered the region in the sixteenth century. In Peru and Bolivia over half the people are of Indian blood, speaking the original Inca language, Quechua.

Lake Titicaca
Outside their reed home on Lake Titicaca, these women are making clothes to be sold at market. Lake Titicaca lies between Peru and Bolivia and is the highest lake in the world.

Life in the Andes
In the southwest of Bolivia lies part of the high Andes mountain range. In this region the average yearly temperature is as low as 39 degrees Fahrenheit. At these high altitudes no trees can survive, and it is too cold to grow crops. The Bolivian people who inhabit this area live by herding llamas, the hardy animals pictured above, which are kept for their wool and meat.

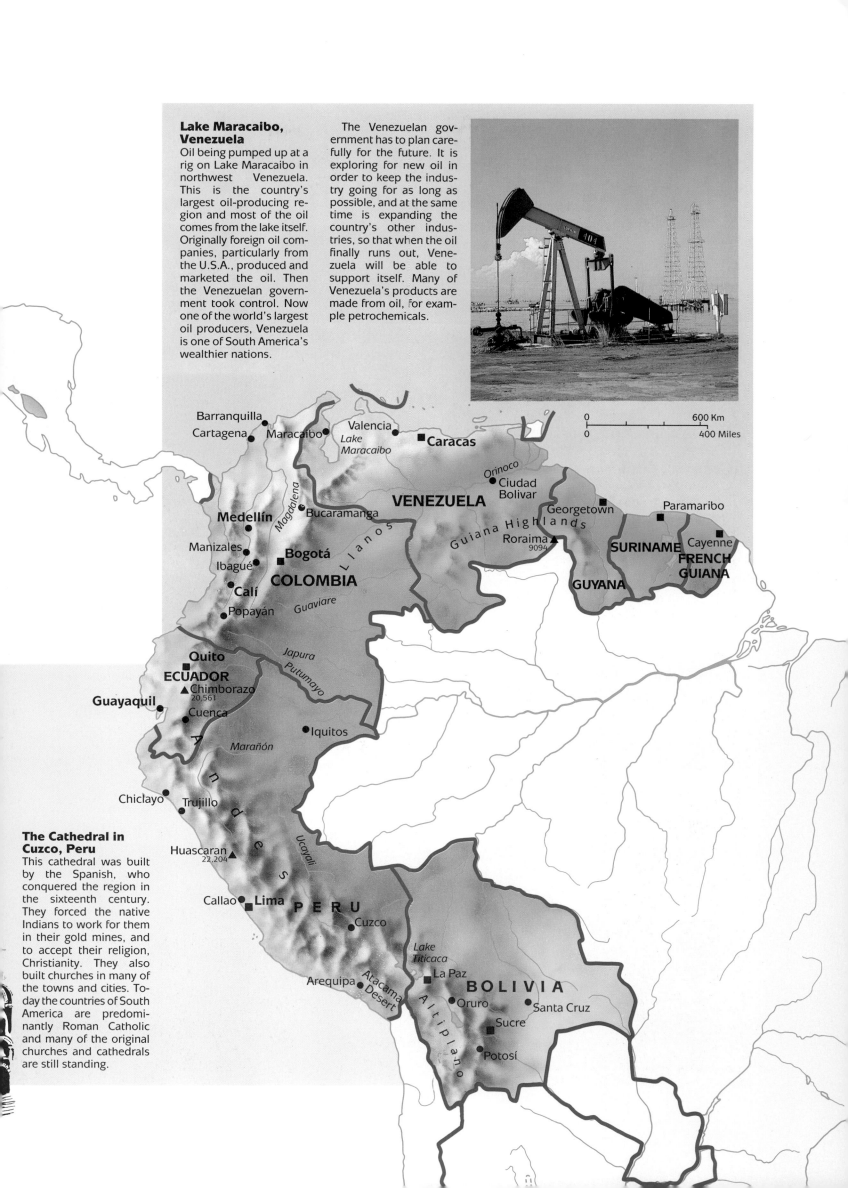

Lake Maracaibo, Venezuela

Oil being pumped up at a rig on Lake Maracaibo in northwest Venezuela. This is the country's largest oil-producing region and most of the oil comes from the lake itself. Originally foreign oil companies, particularly from the U.S.A., produced and marketed the oil. Then the Venezuelan government took control. Now one of the world's largest oil producers, Venezuela is one of South America's wealthier nations.

The Venezuelan government has to plan carefully for the future. It is exploring for new oil in order to keep the industry going for as long as possible, and at the same time is expanding the country's other industries, so that when the oil finally runs out, Venezuela will be able to support itself. Many of Venezuela's products are made from oil, for example petrochemicals.

The Cathedral in Cuzco, Peru

This cathedral was built by the Spanish, who conquered the region in the sixteenth century. They forced the native Indians to work for them in their gold mines, and to accept their religion, Christianity. They also built churches in many of the towns and cities. Today the countries of South America are predominantly Roman Catholic and many of the original churches and cathedrals are still standing.

0   600 Km
0   400 Miles

Barranquilla
Cartagena
Maracaibo
Valencia
Lake Maracaibo
Caracas
Orinoco
Ciudad Bolivar
VENEZUELA
Georgetown
Paramaribo
Magdalena
Bucaramanga
Guiana Highlands
Roraima ▲ 9094
SURINAME
Cayenne
Medellín
FRENCH GUIANA
Manizales
Bogotá
Ibagué
GUYANA
COLOMBIA
Calí
Llanos
Popayán
Guaviare
Japura
Quito
Putumayo
ECUADOR
▲ Chimborazo 20,561
Guayaquil
Cuenca
Iquitos
Marañón
Andes
Chiclayo
Trujillo
Ucayali
Huascaran ▲ 22,204
Callao
Lima
P E R U
Cuzco
Lake Titicaca
La Paz
Arequipa
Atacama Desert
Oruro
Santa Cruz
B O L I V I A
Sucre
Altiplano
Potosí

BRAZIL

B razil is the largest country in South America. For a long time it was governed by Portugal, and Portuguese is still the language spoken by most Brazilians. Brazil is a tropical country and it contains the largest area of tropical rainforest in the world.

The Amazon, the world's second longest river, runs through Brazil. For most of its course it flows through the hot, steamy jungles of the tropical rainforest. In northeast Brazil the climate is dry and farming is difficult, but farther south there are vast grazing lands. Iron ore is mined in the southeast of the country, where coffee and oranges are also produced. These are important exports for Brazil. The main cities are situated in this region. São Paulo is one of South America's most crowded cities, but the beauty of Rio de Janeiro attracts visitors from all over the world. Brazil's capital is Brasilia, a new city that was built so that the government would be situated in the center of the country.

Rio de Janeiro

Rio's carnival is famous throughout the world. Every year during Mardi Gras thousands of people dress in spectacular costumes and parade through the streets. For days on end there is singing and dancing to the rhythms of Brazilian music.

Rainforest

Clearing away the rainforest in Brazil. Every year developers and logging companies destroy rainforest equal to three times the size of Switzerland. Unknown numbers of plants and animals are being lost, and soil washed away.

Brazil's cities

Many people in Brazil's cities live in very poor conditions. Some live in old houses which are ready to collapse.

| 0 | | | 600 Km |
| 0 | | | 400 Miles |

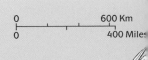

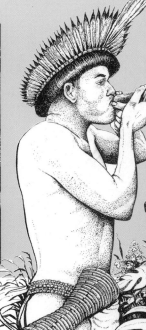

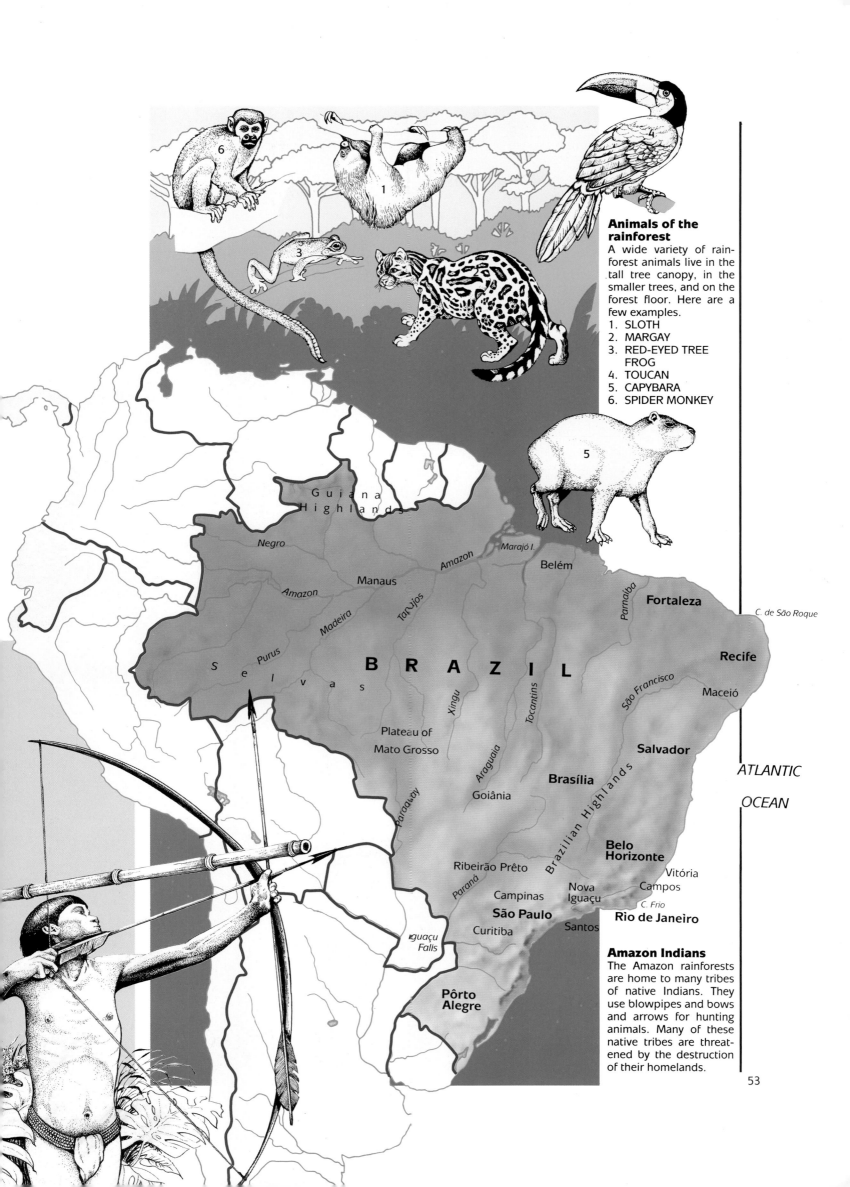

Animals of the rainforest

A wide variety of rainforest animals live in the tall tree canopy, in the smaller trees, and on the forest floor. Here are a few examples.

1. SLOTH
2. MARGAY
3. RED-EYED TREE FROG
4. TOUCAN
5. CAPYBARA
6. SPIDER MONKEY

Amazon Indians

The Amazon rainforests are home to many tribes of native Indians. They use blowpipes and bows and arrows for hunting animals. Many of these native tribes are threatened by the destruction of their homelands.

53

SOUTHERN SOUTH AMERICA

Like much of the continent, many parts of southern South America were conquered by the Spanish in the sixteenth century. Since then immigrants from many European countries have settled there. Some areas, such as the subtropical forests of Paraguay, and the Andes mountains of Chile, still have Indian inhabitants.

Most people live in the large cities: Buenos Aires, the capital of Argentina, is home to one third of Argentina's population, while one half of the people in Uruguay live in its capital, Montevideo. On the vast areas of grassland in Paraguay, Uruguay, and Argentina sheep and cattle are grazed, supplying the meat-packing, wool, and textile industries. Argentina also produces wheat and corn, grown on fields in the Pampas region. In Patagonia, in the south, there are big reserves of oil and gas. Chile has huge mineral deposits, and is one of the world's largest suppliers of copper, which is found in the Atacama Desert in the northern part of the country.

Gauchos
Gauchos are similar to North American cowboys. Traditionally their main job was to take cattle to the markets in the large towns of Argentina, Paraguay, and Uruguay, often riding for several weeks through the grasslands. Today, many of them ride motorbikes and tractors instead of horses.

Chiloé island
The large island of Chiloé lies close to the mainland near Puerto Montt in Chile. The climate is wet and the area prone to earthquakes. The island's port, Castro, was founded in 1567. Many of the houses there are built on stilts in order to raise them clear of soft ground and the flood-water from tidal waves.

Soccer crazy
Soccer is the national sport of most Latin American countries. Uruguay and Argentina have both won the World Cup twice.

The Chilean landscape

Chile, the longest, narrowest country on Earth, is no more than 235 miles wide at any point, but is 2650 miles long, stretching down South America's west coast between the Andes mountains and the Pacific Ocean.

The south of this country is a landscape of lakes, roaring waterfalls, and fuming volcanoes capped with snow, as can be seen in this view of Lake Villarrica. Around Cape Horn, the southernmost tip of South America, lie many thousands of islands and a labyrinth of fjords.

Argentina

In 1816, Argentina declared independence from Spanish rule. Today, it has the second largest population in South America. Its cities are large and cosmopolitan although many of the rural areas are still fairly undeveloped. This picture shows the Plaza de la República in the capital of Argentina, Buenos Aires.

55

EUROPE

This continent is made up of a number of small and densely populated countries. It extends from the Scandinavian countries in the north, which lie partly within the Arctic Circle, to the Mediterranean countries in the south. Also included is the European part of Russia, west of the Ural mountains. Europe contains the world's smallest country, Vatican City, which has fewer than 1000 inhabitants.

Climate and landscape differ enormously, from the cold uplands of Scandinavia and northern Russia, to the semi-desert conditions of parts of central Spain and southern Italy. A range of high mountains crosses southern Europe, forming the Pyrenees between France and Spain, the Alps (which run across Switzerland, France, Austria, Germany, Italy, and Yugoslavia), the Dolomites in Italy, and farther east the Tatra and Carpathian ranges. The highest mountain in

cont. page 58

BELGIUM
Official name Royaume de Belgique
Area 11,783 sq. miles (30,519 sq. km.)
Population 9,875,716
Capital Brussels (pop. 970,346)
Largest cities Antwerp (476,044), Gent (232,620) Charleroi (208,938) Liège (200,312) Bruges (117,857)
Currency Belgian Franc
Official language(s) Dutch (Flemish) and French (Walloon)
Chief products Cement, chemicals, glass, soap, cutlery, paper, steel, textiles, meat products (especially ham and pâté), cereals, dairy products, fish
Exports Iron and steel, textiles, copper, plastic products
Imports Machinery, vehicles, diamonds, oil, food

DENMARK
Official name Kongeriget Danmark
Area 16,638 sq. miles (43,092 sq. km.)
Population 5,129,254
Capital Copenhagen (pop. 468,704)
Largest cities Århus (195,152) Odense (137,286) Ålborg (113,650) Esbjerg (71,112) Randers (55,563) Horsens (46,735)
Currency Danish Krone
Official language(s) Danish
Chief products Dairy products, bacon, poultry, eggs, cereals, livestock, fish, (especially cod, haddock, salmon), cement, diesel engines, electrical equipment, furniture, silverware
Exports Machinery, pork, other meat products, fish
Imports Machinery, manufactured goods, iron and steel, textiles

FRANCE
Official name République Française
Area 210,033 sq. miles (543,965 sq. km.)
Population 55,632,000
Capital Paris (pop. 2,188,918)
Largest cities Marseille (878,689) Lyon (418,476) Toulouse (354,289) Nice (338,486) Strasbourg (252,264)
Currency French Franc
Official language(s) French (Breton and Basque are also spoken)
Chief products Aircraft, vehicles, aluminum, chemicals, electrical equipment, iron and steel, coal, jewelry, perfume, wine, cheese, cereals
Exports Machinery, vehicles, iron and steel, textiles, wheat, oil products, wine, cheese
Imports Machinery, oil, iron and steel, meat, textiles, fruit

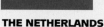

THE NETHERLANDS
Official name Koninkrijk der Nederlanden
Area 15,891 sq. miles (41,160 sq. km.)
Population 14,757,848
Capital Amsterdam (pop. 691,738) (seat of government – The Hague)
Largest cities Rotterdam (574,299) The Hague (444,313) Utrecht (230,373) Eindhoven (191,002) Groningen (167,929)
Currency Guilder
Official language(s) Dutch
Chief products Natural gas, oil, salt, electrical equipment, clothing, iron and steel, machinery, vehicles, ships, dairy products, flowers, cereals
Exports Machinery, textiles, chemical products, meat, flowers, vegetables
Imports Crude oil, vehicles, iron and steel, clothing

UNITED KINGDOM
Official name United Kingdom of Great Britain and Northern Ireland
Area 94,249 sq. miles (244,103 sq. km.)
Population 56,617,900
Capital London (pop. 6,770,400)
Largest cities Birmingham (998,200) Glasgow (715,600) Leeds (709,000) Sheffield (532,300)
Currency Pound Sterling
Official language(s) English
Chief products Oil, natural gas, coal, iron ore, steel, chalk, fish (especially cod, herring), chemicals, clothing, vehicles, cereals, machinery, dairy products
Exports Machinery, vehicles, textiles, electrical equipment, iron and steel, alcoholic drinks, aircraft
Imports Machinery, fruit and vegetables, diamonds, minerals, cereals, butter, meat, textiles

IRELAND
Official name Eire
Area 26,595 sq. miles (68,895 sq. km.)
Population 3,538,000
Capital Dublin
Official language(s) Irish and English
Chief products Processed foods, dairy products, spirits, beer, paper and paper products

ICELAND
Official name Island
Area 39,769 sq. miles (103,000 sq. km.)
Population 300,000
Capital Reykjavik
Official language(s) Icelandic, Danish
Chief products Fish and fish products, cement, aluminum, potatoes, turnips

NORWAY
Official name Kongeriket Norge
Area 125,050 sq. miles (323,878 sq. km.)
Population 4,198,289
Capital Oslo
Official language(s) Norwegian
Chief products Fish (especially cod and herring), lumber, livestock, crude oil, natural gas

SWEDEN
Official name Konungariket Sverige
Area 170,250 sq. miles (440,945 sq. km.)
Population 8,458,880
Capital Stockholm
Official language(s) Swedish
Chief products Aircraft, vehicles, lumber, minerals

FINLAND
Official name Suomen Tasavalta
Area 130,559 sq. miles (338,145 sq. km.)
Population 4,938,602
Capital Helsinki
Official language(s) Finnish and Swedish
Chief products Lumber, paper, textiles, metals

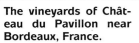

The vineyards of Château du Pavillon near Bordeaux, France.

Europe
Highest point Mount Elbrus (Russia) 18,481ft. (5633m.) above sea level
Lowest point Shore of Caspian Sea 92ft. (28m) below sea level
Longest river Volga River (Russia) 2290mi. (3688km.)
Largest lake Lake Ladoga (Russia) 7100 sq.mi. (18,389 sq.km.)

Málaga (566,330)
Currency Peseta
Official language(s) Spanish (Catalan, Basque and Galician are also spoken)
Chief products Vehicles, cement, iron ore, clothing, ships, steel, olives, wine, grapes, oranges
Exports Machinery, citrus fruits, vegetables, footwear, oil products textiles, ships, olive oil, wine
Imports Crude oil, machinery, iron and steel, organic chemicals, corn, soy, lumber, copper

SPAIN
Official name España
Area 194,897 sq. miles (505,782 sq. km.)
Population 39,400,000
Capital Madrid (pop. 3,124,000)
Largest cities Barcelona (1,703,744)
Valencia (732,471)
Seville (655,435)
Zaragoza (575,317)

ITALY
Official name Repubblica Italiana
Area 116,300 sq. miles (301,225 sq. km.)
Population 57,100,000
Capital Rome (pop. 2,821,420)
Largest cities Milan (1,511,193)
Naples (1,204,959)
Turin (1,034,007)

Genoa (733,990)
Currency Lira
Official language(s) Italian
Chief products Industrial and office equipment, domestic appliances, vehicles, textiles, clothing, chemicals, citrus fruits, wheat, corn, olives, wine
Exports Machinery, textiles, clothing, metals (especially mercury), chemicals, vehicles, footwear, leather goods
Imports Chemicals, metals and minerals, vehicles, agricultural products, food, machinery, oil

PORTUGAL
Official name República Portuguesa
Area 33,370 sq. miles (91,630 sq. km.)
Population 10,350,000
Capital Lisbon
Official language(s) Portuguese
Chief products Ships, textiles, citrus fruits, cork, leather goods, port, fish (especially sardines)

Floating logs downstream in Finland.

Europe is Mont Blanc at 15,771 feet, situated on the border between France and Italy. Many famous rivers flow from these mountains. The Rhine has its source in the Swiss Alps and flows through Germany and the Netherlands. The Danube, which has its source in the Black Forest, flows east through seven countries before reaching the Black Sea.

Much of lowland Europe is intensively cultivated, being given over mostly to cereal crops or dairy herds. Local variations, however, give different regions very distinctive characters: olive groves and vineyards are widespread in countries bordering the Mediterranean or the Black Sea. Fruit orchards and the production of pigs and poultry are common throughout Europe, particularly in areas close to large cities, the major markets for local produce.

Haystacks in the Balkan Mountains in Bulgaria.

UKRAINE
Area 252,046 sq. miles (652,796 sq. km.)
Population 51,200,000
Capital Kiev
Chief products Grain, coal, iron and steel, sugar-beet, machinery, chemicals

GERMANY
Official name Deutschland
Area 137,855 sq. miles (357,042 sq. km.)
Population 77,812,298
Capital Berlin (pop. 3,300,636) (administrative capital – Bonn pop. 276,500)
Currency Deutsche Mark
Official language(s) German
Chief products Minerals, vehicles, steel, chemicals, clothing, electrical goods, livestock, beer, wine

RUSSIA
Area 6,593,391 sq. miles (17,076,811 sq. km.)
Population 145,300,000
Capital Moscow (pop. 8,967,000)
Currency Ruble
Official language(s) Russian, plus 38 minority languages
Chief products Coal, iron ore, minerals, oil, gas, steel, cereals, cotton
See page 83 for information on other former Soviet republics.

LITHUANIA
Area 26,173 sq. miles (67,787 sq. km.)
Population 3,641,000
Capital Vilnius
Chief products Wheat, lumber, potatoes, electrical equipment

GEORGIA
Area 26,911 sq. miles (69,700 sq.km.)
Population 5,449,000
Capital Tbilisi

ARMENIA
Area 11,506 sq. miles (29,800 sq.km.)
Population 3,580,000
Capital Yerevan

ESTONIA
Area 17,413 sq. miles (45,099 sq. km.)
Population 1,556,000
Capital Tallinn

MOLDOVA
Area 13,012 sq. miles (33,700 sq.km.)
Population 4,341,000
Capital Kishniev

CZECHOSLOVAKIA
Area 49,384 sq. miles (127,905 sq. km.)
Population 15,588,177
Capital Prague
Official language(s) Czech and Slovak

POLAND
Area 120,727 sq. miles (312,683 sq. km.)
Population 37,764,300
Capital Warsaw
Official language(s) Polish
Chief products Chemicals, iron, steel, ships, coal

BELARUS
Area 80,300 sq. miles (207,976 sq. km.)
Population 10,259,000
Capital Minsk

LATVIA
Area 24,695 sq. miles (63,959 sq. km.)
Population 2,647,000
Capital Riga

AZERBAIJAN
Area 33,436 sq. miles (88,800 sq.km.)
Population 7,145,600
Capital Baku

The E.C. building in Brussels.

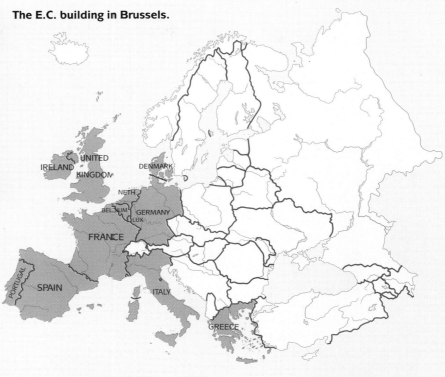

European Community

The European Community is an economic grouping of 12 of the Western European countries. It was formed to promote economic cooperation and coordination between its member states, in order to help them compete on equal terms with the economies of the U.S.A. and Japan. In 1951 the European Coal and Steel Community (E.C.S.C.) was established. This led, in 1957, to the creation of the European Economic Community (E.E.C.) itself.

The European Parliament, formed in 1952, now has 518 members (M.E.P.'s), who are selected in local elections held in each country. The Parliament votes on economic policies relating to trade, agriculture, and environmental issues.

Changes are to be introduced in 1992 which will create a single market within the European Community. Another major policy currently under development is monetary union, which aims to introduce a single currency for use in all of the member countries.

Member countries of the European Community:
Belgium
Denmark
France

Germany
Greece
Ireland
Italy
Luxembourg

The Netherlands
Portugal
Spain
United Kingdom

NAME	AREA SQ. MILES (SQ. KM.)	POPULATION	CAPITAL
Andorra	180 (465)	46,976	Andorra la Vella
Gibraltar (U.K.)	2.125 (6.5)	30,127	–
Liechtenstein	62 (160)	25,215	Vaduz
Malta	122 (316)	345,418	Valletta
Monaco	0.65 (1.6)	27,063	Monaco
San Marino	23.4 (60.5)	19,149	San Marino
The Vatican City	0.17 (0.44)	1000	

ANDORRA   MALTA

MONACO   VATICAN CITY

Note: Cyprus is defined here as part of Europe but appears also on the maps of Asia on pages 85 and 87. For Turkey's flag and details, see page 86.

LUXEMBOURG
Area 998 sq. miles (2,585 sq. km.)
Population 367,200
Capital Luxembourg
Official language(s) French, Letzeburgish
Chief products Chemicals, iron, machinery, paints

SWITZERLAND
Area 15,943 sq. miles (41,293 sq. km.)
Population 6,566,799
Capital Bern
Official language(s) German, French, Italian
Chief products Electrical equipment, chemicals

AUSTRIA
Area 32,377 sq. miles (83,855 sq. km.)
Population 7,576,000
Capital Vienna
Official language(s) German
Chief products Lumber, chemicals, iron ore and steel

YUGOSLAVIA
Area 98,766 sq. miles (255,804 sq. km.)
Population 23,411,000
Capital Belgrade
Official language(s) Serbo-Croat
Chief products Chemicals, metal products, copper

HUNGARY
Area 35,920 sq. miles (93,033 sq. km.)
Population 10,604,000
Capital Budapest
Official language(s) Hungarian
Chief products Coal, bauxite, wheat, sugar beet

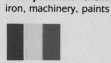
ROMANIA
Area 91,699 sq. miles (237,500 sq. km.)
Population 22,940,430
Capital Bucharest
Official language(s) Romanian
Chief products Iron ore, oil, natural gas, machinery

BULGARIA
Area 42,823 sq. miles (110,912 sq. km.)
Population 8,973,596
Capital Sofia
Official language(s) Bulgarian
Chief products Cereals, electrical equipment, fruit

GREECE
Area 50,949 sq. miles (131,957 sq. km.)
Population 9,990,000
Capital Athens
Official language(s) Greek
Chief products Bauxite, lignite, cotton, tobacco citrus fruits, olives, textiles

ALBANIA
Area 11,100 sq. miles (28,748 sq. km.)
Population 3,082,700
Capital Tiranë
Official language(s) Albanian
Chief products Textiles, oil products, wheat

CYPRUS
Area 3572 sq. miles (9251 sq. km.)
Population 673,000
Capital Nicosia
Official language(s) Greek and Turkish
Chief products Clothing, footwear, plastics, avocados

SCANDINAVIA AND FINLAND

The countries of Scandinavia (Norway, Sweden, and Denmark), together with Finland and the island of Iceland, lie in the north of Europe. These countries have small populations and a high standard of living.

Norway, Sweden, and Finland are all heavily forested, so logging — the felling of trees to make paper, furniture, and other wood-based products — is an important industry. The warming influence of the Atlantic Gulf Stream brings with it huge shoals of cod, haddock, mackerel, and herring; Norway, Denmark, and Iceland all have large fishing industries. Norway has also benefited from the discovery, in 1970, of oil in the North Sea. Valuable supplies of iron ore and other minerals in Sweden supply its heavy industry, which produces ships, Volvo and Saab cars, and airplanes.

Iceland's volcanoes and geysers attract many tourists during the short summer, and much of this volcanic power is harnessed to produce electricity.

Danish farming
Cheesemaking in Denmark. Danish agriculture is centered on cattle, pigs, and chickens, and most of the crops grown in Denmark are used to feed the livestock.

Swedish logging mill
Trees are cut in the forests of Sweden and floated downstream to a logging mill where they are processed into pulp. This is then used to make paper.

A Norwegian fishing port
Sea fishing is one of Norway's most important industries. All the way up its long indented coastline there are fishing ports like this one, Hammerfest, in the far north of Norway.

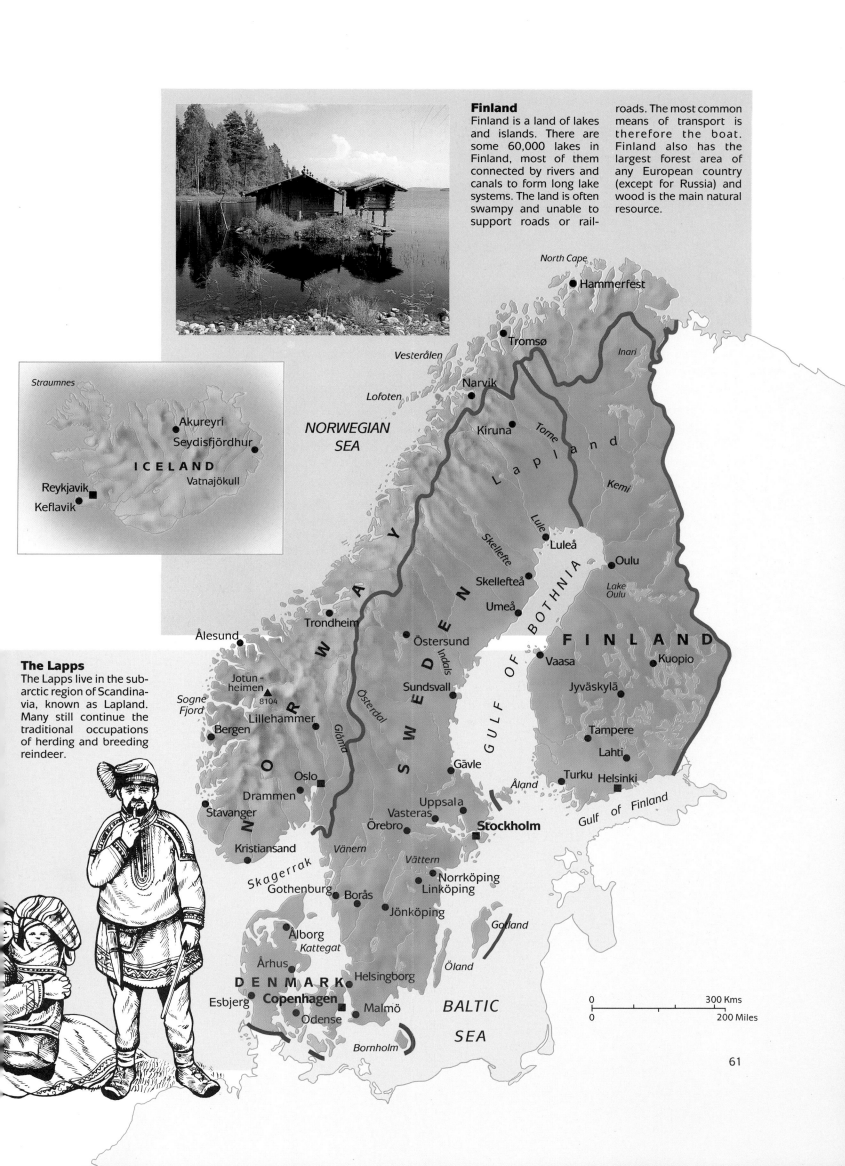

Finland

Finland is a land of lakes and islands. There are some 60,000 lakes in Finland, most of them connected by rivers and canals to form long lake systems. The land is often swampy and unable to support roads or railroads. The most common means of transport is therefore the boat. Finland also has the largest forest area of any European country (except for Russia) and wood is the main natural resource.

The Lapps

The Lapps live in the sub-arctic region of Scandinavia, known as Lapland. Many still continue the traditional occupations of herding and breeding reindeer.

North Cape

Hammerfest

Tromsø

Vesterålen

Narvik

Inari

Lofoten

NORWEGIAN SEA

Kiruna

Lapland

Torne

Kemi

Straumnes

Akureyri

Seydisfjördhur

ICELAND

Vatnajökull

Reykjavik

Keflavik

Lule

Skellefte

Luleå

Oulu

Skellefteå

Lake Oulu

Umeå

GULF OF BOTHNIA

FINLAND

Trondheim

Ålesund

Östersund

Vaasa

Kuopio

Indals

Jyväskylä

Jotun-heimen

Sogne Fjord

8104

Sundsvall

Österdal

SWEDEN

NORWAY

Lillehammer

Bergen

Glåma

Tampere

Lahti

Gävle

Turku

Helsinki

Oslo

Åland

Drammen

Vasteras

Uppsala

Gulf of Finland

Stavanger

Örebro

Stockholm

Kristiansand

Vänern

Vättern

Skagerrak

Norrköping

Linköping

Gothenburg

Borås

Jönköping

Gotland

Ålborg

Kattegat

Öland

Århus

Helsingborg

DENMARK

Esbjerg

Copenhagen

Malmö

BALTIC SEA

Odense

Bornholm

| 0 | | 300 Kms |
| 0 | | 200 Miles |

61

BRITISH ISLES

The British Isles consist of the two main islands of Great Britain and Ireland, and a number of much smaller islands. The United Kingdom is made up of England, Wales, Scotland, and Northern Ireland.

The position of the British Isles, near the warming influence of the Atlantic Gulf Stream, gives a mild climate. Cereal and vegetable crops grow well in the lowlands of southern England, while upland pastures in western and northern regions provide grazing for sheep and dairy cattle.

Britain's heavy industry grew up around the coalfields of central Scotland, northern England, and south Wales. Shipbuilding, textile, and steelmaking industries were centered on cities such as Glasgow, Newcastle, and Manchester, and Belfast in Northern Ireland. Now, half of Britain's exports come from the manufacture of electrical and engineering equipment, such as airplane engines, cars, tractors, and electronic devices. London, the capital of England, is a financial center of international importance.

The Lloyds Building, London
The new Lloyds Building, built in 1986, houses the world's most famous insurance company. The company originated in 1688 in Edward Lloyd's coffeehouse.

County Kerry, Ireland
The low green fields of central Ireland gradually rise to the high peaks on the southwestern coast. The most westerly point in the British Isles is in County Kerry, where the full force of the Atlantic Ocean has made a rugged, indented coastline with high-sided river estuaries. Ireland's countryside has remained unspoilt because it is not heavily industrialized.

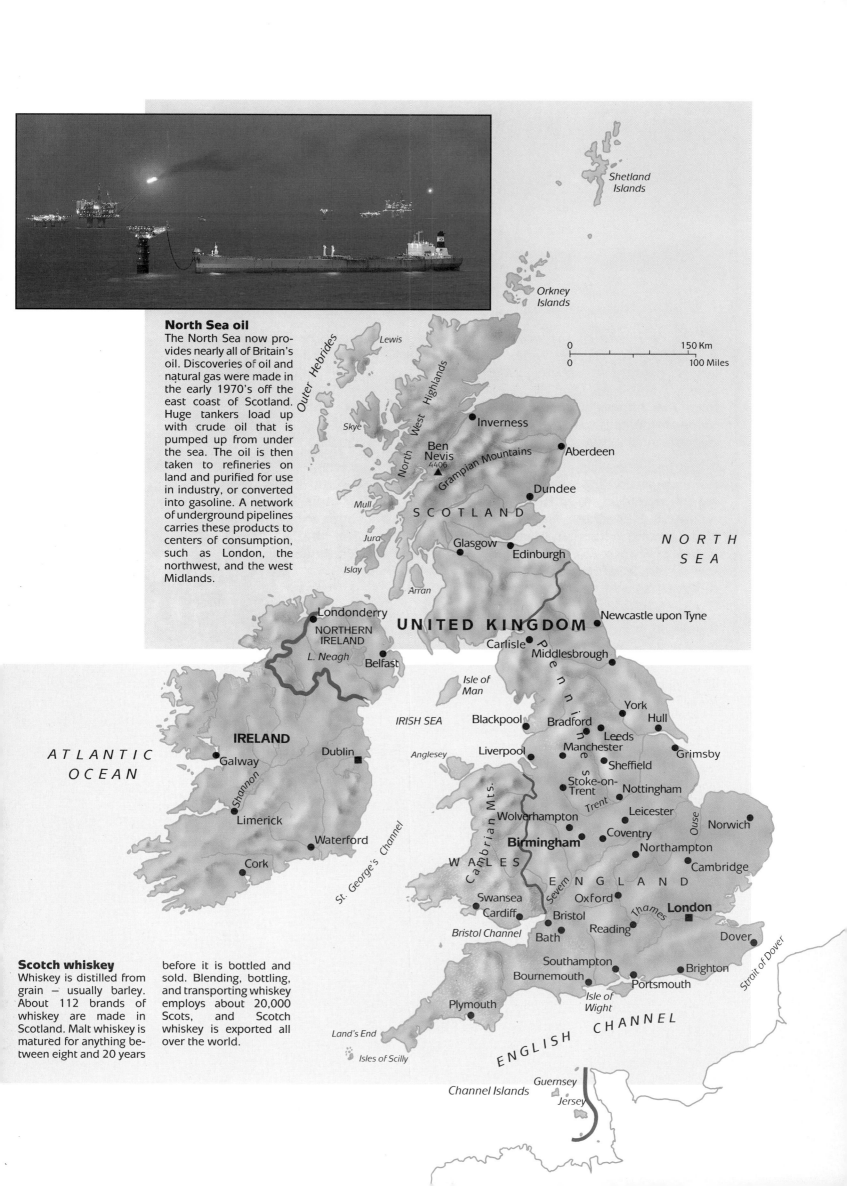

North Sea oil

The North Sea now provides nearly all of Britain's oil. Discoveries of oil and natural gas were made in the early 1970's off the east coast of Scotland. Huge tankers load up with crude oil that is pumped up from under the sea. The oil is then taken to refineries on land and purified for use in industry, or converted into gasoline. A network of underground pipelines carries these products to centers of consumption, such as London, the northwest, and the west Midlands.

Scotch whiskey

Whiskey is distilled from grain — usually barley. About 112 brands of whiskey are made in Scotland. Malt whiskey is matured for anything between eight and 20 years before it is bottled and sold. Blending, bottling, and transporting whiskey employs about 20,000 Scots, and Scotch whiskey is exported all over the world.

Shetland Islands

Orkney Islands

150 Km
100 Miles

Outer Hebrides

Lewis

Skye

North West Highlands

Inverness

Ben Nevis 4406 ▲ Grampian Mountains

Aberdeen

Mull

Dundee

Jura

SCOTLAND

Islay

Glasgow

Edinburgh

Arran

NORTH SEA

Londonderry

NORTHERN IRELAND

L. Neagh

Belfast

UNITED KINGDOM

Newcastle upon Tyne

Carlisle

Middlesbrough

Isle of Man

Pennines

IRISH SEA

Blackpool

Bradford

York

Hull

IRELAND

Dublin

Anglesey

Liverpool

Leeds

Manchester

Sheffield

Grimsby

ATLANTIC OCEAN

Galway

Shannon

Stoke-on-Trent

Nottingham

Trent

Leicester

Limerick

Cambrian Mts.

Wolverhampton

Coventry

Northampton

Ouse

Norwich

Waterford

Birmingham

WALES

ENGLAND

Cambridge

Cork

St. George's Channel

Severn

Oxford

Thames

London

Swansea

Cardiff

Bristol

Reading

Dover

Bristol Channel

Bath

Strait of Dover

Southampton

Brighton

Bournemouth

Portsmouth

Plymouth

Isle of Wight

Land's End

ENGLISH CHANNEL

Isles of Scilly

Guernsey

Channel Islands

Jersey

FRANCE

France is one of the richest nations in Europe, and is famous for its fine wines and good cooking. It is the largest country in Western Europe and 90 percent of its land is suitable for farming. The mild temperatures and rain from the Atlantic Ocean, and farther south the warmer Mediterranean climate, provide suitable conditions for the cultivation of wheat, corn, artichokes, grapes, and tobacco.

The main industrial region lies in the northeast where there are important steel and engineering industries, including the manufacture of Renault and Citroën cars. But there are also newer centers for high-tech industry in the south, in areas around Toulouse, Marseille, and Grenoble. Paris, the capital of France, has been a world center of art and learning for hundreds of years. Today, it is also well known for designer fashion, and for its perfume industry.

France is a country of widely differing landscapes. The French Alps are popular for skiing, while the Riviera along the Mediterranean coast is a fashionable beach resort.

The Louvre

The Louvre in Paris was once one of the palaces of the kings of France. Today it is an art gallery, full of famous paintings, including Leonardo da Vinci's *Mona Lisa*, sculpture, and antiquities. This glass pyramid is the latest addition to the Louvre buildings, forming a new entrance hall. It was commissioned by the French president, François Mitterrand.

The T.G.V. Atlantique

The T.G.V. Atlantique is the first train in the world to travel at 185 miles per hour. New railroads have been specially laid for the train which runs from Paris to the Atlantic coast in two hours. It is part of a modern network of high-speed railroads which will eventually link up with Brussels, Amsterdam, Cologne, and London via the Channel Tunnel. The picture on the right shows the new T.G.V. being constructed.

French wine

Grape cultivation is a cherished occupation in France. Each September the grapes are picked and taken to the presses. The grape juice slowly turns into high quality wines such as Champagne, Burgundy, and Bordeaux, which are named after the regions they come from. French wines are exported all over the world.

The Tour de France

The Tour de France is the most popular sporting event in France. For three weeks in July, 150 cyclists race around France, climbing steep mountain roads and enduring high temperatures. A trail of TV camera crews, reporters, trainers, and emergency services follows, and crowds line the route to offer their support.

Boulogne
Lille
Somme
Cherbourg
Le Havre
Amiens
P i c a r d y
Rouen
Oise
Caen
Reims
Meuse
N o r m a n d y
Marne
Metz
Nancy
Paris
Brest
C h a m p a g n e
B r i t t a n y
Seine
Vosges
Quimper
Troyes
Strasbourg
Rennes
Plateau de Langres
Le Mans
Orléans
Yonne
Auxerre
Mulhouse
Angers
Loire
St.Nazaire
Tours
Doubs
Cher
Dijon
Besançon
Nantes
Bourges
B u r g u n d y
Poitiers
F R A N C E
Jura Mts.
La Rochelle
Vienne
Saône
B A Y
Roanne
O F
Mt.
B I S C A Y
Limoges
Clermont-
Blanc
15,771
Ferrand
Angoulême
Puy de Sancy
6,85
Lyon
A
Périgueux
Allier
St.-Étienne
Grenoble
l
Dordogne
M a s s i f
Bordeaux
p
Valence
C e n t r a l
s
Lot
Garonne
Rhône
G a s c o n y
Nîmes
Avignon
Nice
Bayonne
Durance
Cannes
MONACO
Toulouse
Montpellier
Pau
Riviera
Béziers
Marseille
Toulon
P y r e n e e s
Bastia
Perpignan
M E D I T E R R A N E A N
S E A
Corsica
0   200 Km
0   150 Miles
Ajaccio

BENELUX

Benelux is a name given to a group of three countries: BElgium, the NEtherlands (often known as Holland), and LUXembourg. The landscape of Holland and parts of Belgium is very flat, crisscrossed by canals and waterways. About 3000 square miles of land in Holland have been reclaimed from the sea by draining away the water and building dikes and dams to keep the seawater out. Almost all the land is used for agriculture, specializing in dairy farming and horticulture.

All the Benelux countries are densely populated. Belgium is split between Dutch- and Flemish-speaking Flemings in the north, and French speaking Walloons in the south. A large proportion of these people work in industry. Despite the fact that most raw materials have to be imported, both Belgium and Luxembourg have heavy and light industries, producing metals, textiles, and chemicals as well as more specialized items such as soap and cutlery.

Esch-sur-Sûre
The Sûre River cuts its path through the wooded hills around Esch-sur-Sûre in northern Luxembourg. This region of Luxembourg and the Ardennes region in southeast Belgium are well known for their beautiful natural scenery. Groves of walnut trees hide slate-roofed villages and remote castles. The Ardennes region is also renowned for its ham and pâté.

Rotterdam

Rotterdam is the world's busiest port. It is situated at the mouth of the Rhine and Maas rivers which serve the industrial heartlands of Europe. Goods from the industrial Ruhr region of Germany, for example, are taken downstream by barge to Rotterdam where they are lifted by crane on to oceangoing vessels. Huge oil tankers arrive from the Middle East bringing crude oil for the oil refineries and the many related petrochemical plants that are located here. The Dutch oil company, Shell, can now send oil by pipeline direct from its refinery at the harbor to Amsterdam, Antwerp, and Germany. However, it is shipbuilding that is the most important industry in Rotterdam. Ever since the seventeenth century when the Dutch started trading with the Far East, skilled craftworkers have been building merchant vessels. Today, their expertise is sought throughout the world by countries that need large container ships and supertankers.

Alkmaar cheese market

Alkmaar, a town near Amsterdam, is famous for its cheese market. Every Friday from April to October cheeses are put on display by cheeseporters who still wear a traditional costume dating from the sixteenth century. Alkmaar is a center for the dairy industry which is the main form of agriculture in the Netherlands. The warm waters of the Gulf Stream bring mild winters and wet summers which help to produce a long growing season and excellent grazing land for cattle.

The Atomium

The Atomium is an aluminum structure that was built for the World Fair in 1958 in Brussels. It is intended to represent a molecule of an iron crystal, magnified 265 million times. Each sphere is an atom, making up a total of nine atoms in the molecule. The three lower atoms now house an exhibition on the peaceful use of nuclear energy. You can take escalators up the tubes to reach a restaurant in the top sphere.

GERMANY

After World War II Germany was divided into two — the Federal Republic of Germany (West Germany) and the German Democratic Republic (East Germany), which traded almost exclusively with other Eastern European countries. In 1989, restrictions on freedom of travel and communication between the two countries were lifted for the first time since the war, and Germany was officially united on October 3, 1990.

Germany is a leading industrial nation. It has large natural reserves of coal and iron ore, and the Ruhr valley is one of the most important industrial centers in Europe. The Rhine is a vital route for industrial cargo, handled by ports such as Mannheim, Cologne, and Duisburg. Germany also has traditional centers of manufacturing such as Dresden, famous for its china.

The northern region of Germany is a lowland plain — farther south the land is more mountainous and heavily forested. The coniferous forests and remote castles of the Black Forest and Bavarian Alps attract many tourists.

Coal cutting in the Ruhr
Lignite, also known as brown coal, is being excavated at this open-cast mine in the Ruhr district. Modern equipment can dig out the coal quickly and efficiently. The Ruhr is one of the largest industrial areas in Europe.

Rothenburg on the Tauber
Rothenburg on the Tauber is in Bavaria in the south of Germany. It is one of the best preserved medieval towns in Germany, and little has changed in 400 years. All its walls, towers, high-gabled houses and narrow crooked streets date from that time. Traditional crafts such as woodcarving are still practiced.

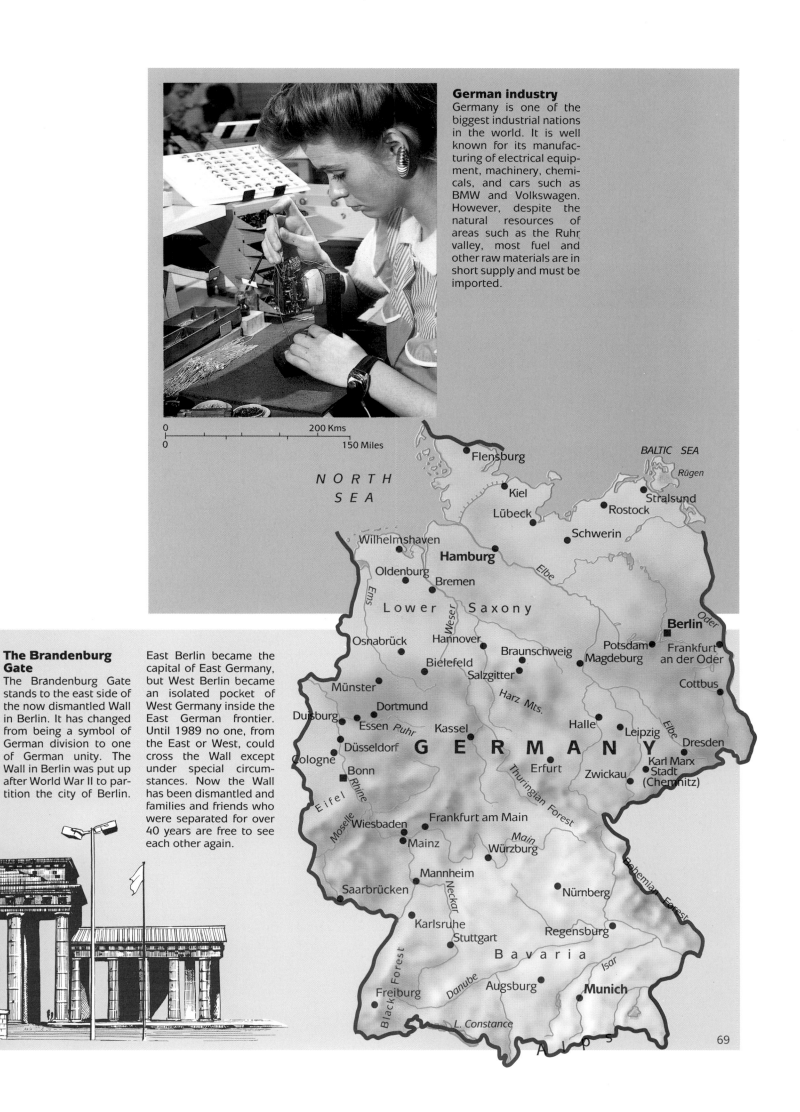

German industry

Germany is one of the biggest industrial nations in the world. It is well known for its manufacturing of electrical equipment, machinery, chemicals, and cars such as BMW and Volkswagen. However, despite the natural resources of areas such as the Ruhr valley, most fuel and other raw materials are in short supply and must be imported.

The Brandenburg Gate

The Brandenburg Gate stands to the east side of the now dismantled Wall in Berlin. It has changed from being a symbol of German division to one of German unity. The Wall in Berlin was put up after World War II to partition the city of Berlin.

East Berlin became the capital of East Germany, but West Berlin became an isolated pocket of West Germany inside the East German frontier. Until 1989 no one, from the East or West, could cross the Wall except under special circumstances. Now the Wall has been dismantled and families and friends who were separated for over 40 years are free to see each other again.

0   200 Kms
0   150 Miles

NORTH SEA

BALTIC SEA

Rügen

Flensburg

Kiel

Stralsund

Lübeck

Rostock

Schwerin

Wilhelmshaven

Oldenburg

Bremen

Hamburg

Elbe

Ems

Lower Saxony

Weser

Osnabrück

Hannover

Braunschweig

Berlin

Oder

Bielefeld

Salzgitter

Potsdam

Magdeburg

Frankfurt an der Oder

Münster

Harz Mts.

Cottbus

Dortmund

Duisburg

Essen

Ruhr

Kassel

Halle

Leipzig

Elbe

Dresden

Düsseldorf

GERMANY

Cologne

Bonn

Erfurt

Zwickau

Karl Marx Stadt (Chemnitz)

Thuringian Forest

Eifel

Rhine

Moselle

Wiesbaden

Frankfurt am Main

Main

Mainz

Würzburg

Bohemian Forest

Mannheim

Saarbrücken

Neckar

Nürnberg

Karlsruhe

Regensburg

Stuttgart

Bavaria

Isar

Black Forest

Freiburg

Danube

Augsburg

Munich

L. Constance

Alps

AUSTRIA AND SWITZERLAND

Austria and Switzerland are the most mountainous countries in Europe, with the Alps covering three quarters of their land. Much of the people's way of life is dictated by this environment.

Since the sixteenth century Switzerland has had a policy of neutrality in times of war. This reputation for neutrality and security has made Switzerland one of the world's most important centers for banking.

Neither Austria nor Switzerland has reserves of oil or coal, and as a result water power from the mountain rivers is a vital source of energy. Austria also relies heavily on Eastern European countries for its energy supplies. Swiss workers make high-quality products such as watches and scientific instruments, while Austria has big chemical and manufacturing industries. Tourism is extremely important in both countries: there are many famous ski resorts, and Vienna, the capital of Austria, is one of the great cultural centers of the world.

Swiss commerce
Switzerland has long had a tradition of neutrality and security. As a result it has become an important center for international commerce and banking. The Swiss city Geneva is also the European headquarters for international organizations such as the Red Cross and the United Nations, and it has often been used by other countries to stage peace talks.

Ski school at Verbier

Most Swiss children feel at home on skis by the age of seven. Local primary schools give lessons on the slopes, and there are special ski schools to develop technique at an early age. Verbier is a big ski resort which attracts skiers from all over Europe every winter.

The Tirol

The far western arm of Austria is part of a region known as the Tirol. It is one of the highest Alpine areas and also one of the most traditional. The province was founded in the fourteenth century and is still regarded by its inhabitants as distinct from the modern states of Austria and Italy across which it lies.

Prater Park

This fairground wheel in Prater Park in Vienna, the capital of Austria, is one of the largest in Europe.

Salzburg

Salzburg lies just inside the border between Austria and Germany. It is the birthplace of the famous composer, Wolfgang Amadeus Mozart. Every summer there is a music festival in celebration of Mozart's operas and chamber music. Thousands of people come from all over Europe to enjoy the festival, and all the restaurants and hotels are full.

ITALY

Italy juts into the Mediterranean Sea and includes the two islands of Sicily at its foot, and Sardinia to the west. It is one of the youngest countries in Europe — its various kingdoms were not united until 1870.

Italy ranks among the richer nations of the world, yet there is a huge difference between the standard of living in the prosperous, industrial north and the poorer, mainly agricultural south. Rome may be the capital of Italy, but Milan in the north is its business, financial, and industrial capital, and an international center for fashion and design. In addition trades such as glassblowing, shoemaking, and weaving textiles for high-quality clothes are still practiced in various traditional centers. However, Italy has limited natural resources and imports both oil and electricity.

In the south, olives and citrus fruits are grown, but the most fertile agricultural area is the Po valley in the north. Grapes are grown on the slopes of the Apennine mountains.

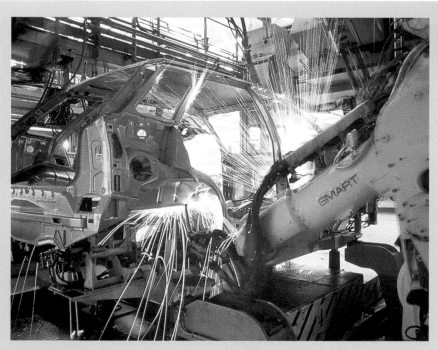

Italy's industry
Italy's biggest manufacturing company is Fiat Motor Cars based in Turin. This company has one of the most up-to-date methods of car production in the world. Robots are used for complete precision in every process — assembling, welding, and painting.

Vatican City
The Vatican is a separate city within Rome, from where the Pope leads the Roman Catholic Church worldwide. As well as being the smallest country in the world, with an area of less than one square mile, it is also the only place where Latin is the official language. It has its own bank, telephone, and postal system as well as a small army called the Swiss Guard to protect the Pope himself.

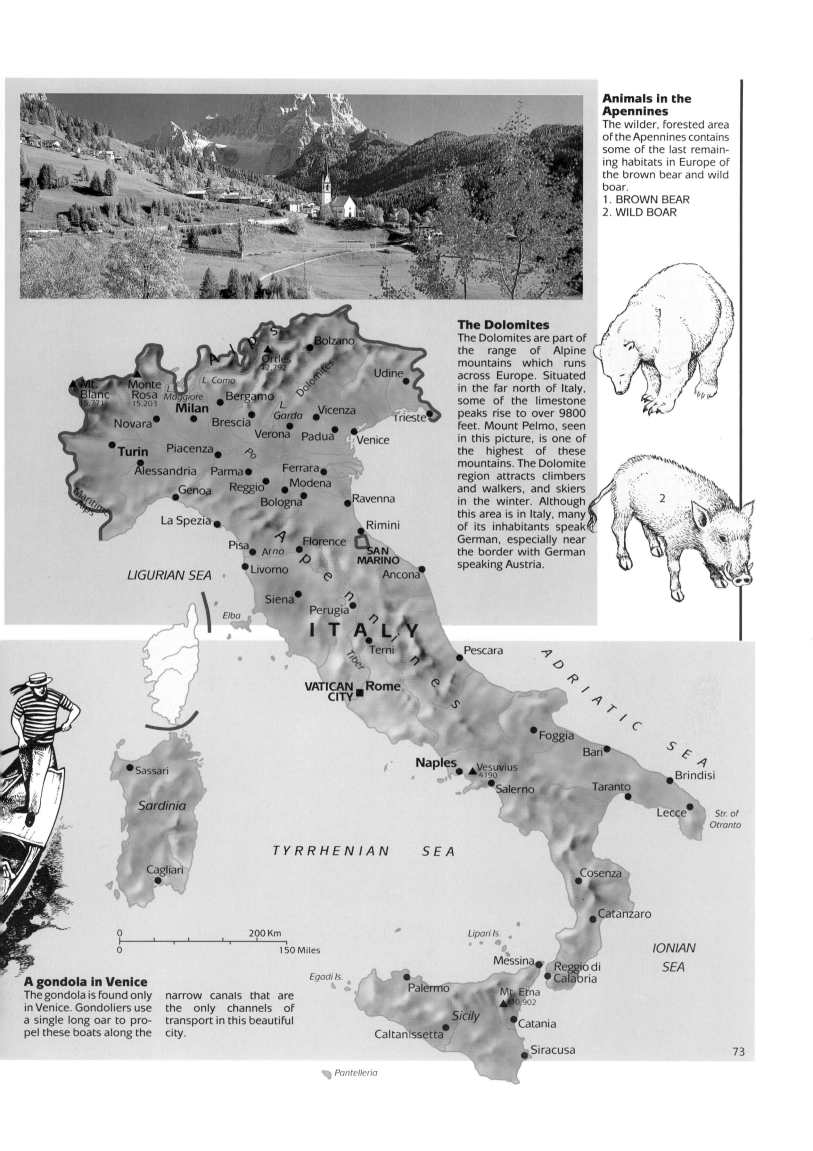

Animals in the Apennines
The wilder, forested area of the Apennines contains some of the last remaining habitats in Europe of the brown bear and wild boar.
1. BROWN BEAR
2. WILD BOAR

The Dolomites
The Dolomites are part of the range of Alpine mountains which runs across Europe. Situated in the far north of Italy, some of the limestone peaks rise to over 9800 feet. Mount Pelmo, seen in this picture, is one of the highest of these mountains. The Dolomite region attracts climbers and walkers, and skiers in the winter. Although this area is in Italy, many of its inhabitants speak German, especially near the border with German speaking Austria.

A gondola in Venice
The gondola is found only in Venice. Gondoliers use a single long oar to propel these boats along the narrow canals that are the only channels of transport in this beautiful city.

A L P S
Bolzano
Ortles 12,792
Udine
L. Como
Mt. Blanc 15,771
Monte Rosa 15,203
L. Maggiore
Bergamo
Dolomites
Milan
L. Garda
Vicenza
Trieste
Novara
Brescia
Verona
Padua
Venice
Turin
Piacenza
Po
Alessandria
Parma
Ferrara
Genoa
Reggio
Modena
Bologna
Ravenna
Maritime Alps
La Spezia
Rimini
A
p
e
n
n
i
n
e
s
Florence
SAN MARINO
Pisa
Arno
Ancona
Livorno
Siena
Perugia
ITALY
Elba
Terni
Pescara
Tiber
VATICAN CITY
Rome
ADRIATIC SEA
LIGURIAN SEA
Foggia
Bari
Naples
Vesuvius 4190
Brindisi
Taranto
Salerno
Lecce
Str. of Otranto
Sassari
Cosenza
Sardinia
Catanzaro
Cagliari
TYRRHENIAN SEA
IONIAN SEA
Lipari Is.
Messina
Reggio di Calabria
Egadi Is.
Palermo
Mt. Etna 10,902
Sicily
Catania
Caltanissetta
Siracusa
Pantelleria

0   200 Km
0   150 Miles

SPAIN AND PORTUGAL

In the southwest corner of Europe, Spain and Portugal form the Iberian Peninsula. Spain is the second largest country in western Europe but it has only the fifth largest population. Spanish is one of four languages spoken — and almost a quarter of the Spanish speakers use dialects other than the offical Castilian Spanish.

Since 1930 much of the Spanish population has moved away from the countryside to live and work in the main cities and industrial centers. The chemical industry, shipbuilding, steel production, and tourism are all important for Spain's economy. Spain also exports agricultural products, including olive oil, citrus fruit, and sherry from the Jerez region.

Portugal is less developed than Spain, but industry is now becoming more important. Tourism and the export of textiles are the traditional mainstays; in addition most of Europe's supply of cork comes from special oak trees in the south of the country.

Olive groves in Andalusia
Olives, which need little water, grow well in Andalusia in the south of Spain, where it is hot and dry. Most are crushed to make olive oil.

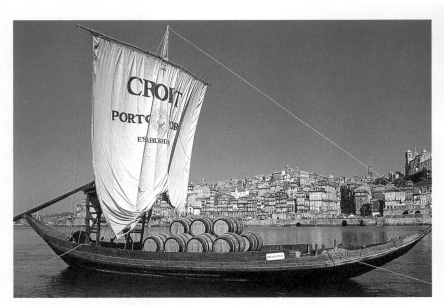

Oporto port
Portugal is famous for its port, a dark red wine usually drunk after dinner. It is made at vineyards along the Douro River, then put into casks and taken downstream by barge to Oporto, the city after which the wine is named. Here, the port is stored in cellars, called "Lodges," and may be left to mature for ten to twenty years before being shipped all over the world.

Bullfighting
Every Sunday evening in Spain during the summer, crowds assemble in bullrings around the country. They watch and cheer as their favorite matador flicks his scarlet cape at the charging bull.

74

Spanish animals

The Spanish lynx is a long-legged wild cat that lives in the forest and preys on birds and small mammals. Red foxes are common in much of Europe.
1. SPANISH LYNX
2. RED FOX

Bilbao

Bilbao is a major Spanish port situated in northern Spain. Iron ore was discovered in Bilbao in the nineteenth century, and the town fast became an industrial center with iron and steel foundries and shipbuilding yards. Bilbao is also the center for the Basque movement ETA *(Euskadi ta Askatasuna,* meaning Freedom for the Basque Homeland), which agitates for independence from Spain.

SOUTHEAST EUROPE

Yugoslavia, Romania, Bulgaria, Greece, and Albania are known as the Balkan countries. They lie at the extreme southeast of Europe, close to Asia. In the past many different European and Asian peoples have settled in this area, resulting in the present mixture of people, languages, and religions.

Much of the region is mountainous. The river Danube, which forms the boundary between Romania and Bulgaria before flowing into the Black Sea, is surrounded by fertile, heavily-cultivated land. Much of the produce is sold in local markets but Bulgaria exports agricultural goods such as canned fruits and vegetables, and Greece exports olive oil and citrus fruits.

Heavy industry plays an important part in the economies of these countries; Bulgaria also has a fast-growing electronics industry. Yugoslavia is the leading European producer of copper, while Greece is a shipping center. Tourism is also extremely important, especially for Greece.

A fruit market in Dubrovnik
Dubrovnik is an old walled seaport on the Adriatic coast of Yugoslavia. It is also a market center for products such as cheese, milk, wood, olives, and grapes brought from neighboring villages.

Meteora, Greece
There are many monasteries in the beautiful mountainous country-side of Greece. The monasteries at Meteora in central Greece are set on top of a pinnacle of rock. To reach them, before steps were cut, people were hauled up the side in a basket.

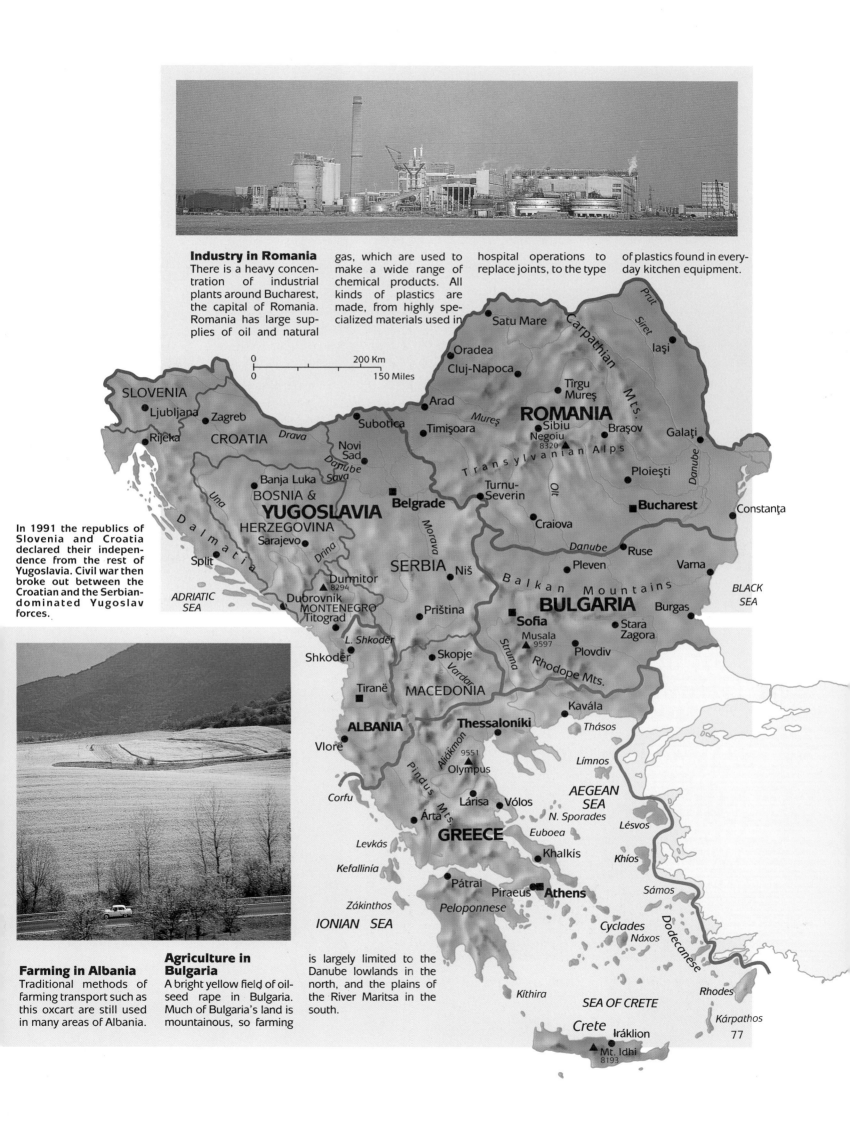

Industry in Romania

There is a heavy concentration of industrial plants around Bucharest, the capital of Romania. Romania has large supplies of oil and natural gas, which are used to make a wide range of chemical products. All kinds of plastics are made, from highly specialized materials used in hospital operations to replace joints, to the type of plastics found in everyday kitchen equipment.

In 1991 the republics of Slovenia and Croatia declared their independence from the rest of Yugoslavia. Civil war then broke out between the Croatian and the Serbian-dominated Yugoslav forces.

Farming in Albania

Traditional methods of farming transport such as this oxcart are still used in many areas of Albania.

Agriculture in Bulgaria

A bright yellow field of oil-seed rape in Bulgaria. Much of Bulgaria's land is mountainous, so farming is largely limited to the Danube lowlands in the north, and the plains of the River Maritsa in the south.

77

CENTRAL EUROPE

Czechoslovakia, Poland, and Hungary form part of central Europe. Poland and Hungary are both mainly lowland countries, and Hungary is heavily forested. Czechoslovakia is more mountainous. The climate throughout this region is temperate, but winters can be extremely cold, and ice often closes the harbors along the Polish Baltic coast.

Poland and Czechoslovakia are rich in natural resources and are both heavily industrialized. Poland mines coal, mainly from coalfields in Silesia, which is both exported and used to supply the steel and shipbuilding industries based around Gdansk on the Baltic coast. Large deposits of gold were found in Czechoslovakia in the mid-1980's; uranium is also mined in the mountains and used to produce nuclear power.

South of Budapest, the beautiful capital city of Hungary, the land surrounding the River Danube is particularly fertile, and crops such as wheat, sugar beet, and potatoes are grown.

Refining oil
This maze of pipes and tanks is necessary for the complex process of oil production. Czechoslovakia, Poland, and Hungary do not have large natural reserves of oil, so all three countries are forced to import crude oil from abroad. When crude oil is taken from below the ground or sea it has to be refined, so that it can be separated into oil, gasoline, paraffin, and other products. This oil refinery is in Szazhalombatta, near Budapest, the capital of Hungary.

Polish traditional dress
In some rural areas Polish men and women still wear traditional dress. The strong, well-made garments last for a long time. These costumes are also worn for festivals and folkdances which are an important part of popular culture all over Eastern Europe. Especially in the rural areas, traditional customs have been passed down from generation to generation and kept alive.

Charles Bridge, Prague
The city of Prague, capital of Czechoslovakia, was a major European cultural center in medieval times. Much of the beautiful architecture remains, and now the old palaces house government institutions and academies of music and art.

Agriculture in Poland

Rolling green fields typical of Poland's central agricultural region. Most of the farmland is planted with crops to grow feed for pigs and chickens. Farming machinery is usually old fashioned and frequently there are no fertilizers to help crops grow in the poorer soils. Distribution of farm produce to the market centers can also be difficult. There are sometimes food shortages and people often have to line up for hours to buy meat or bread.

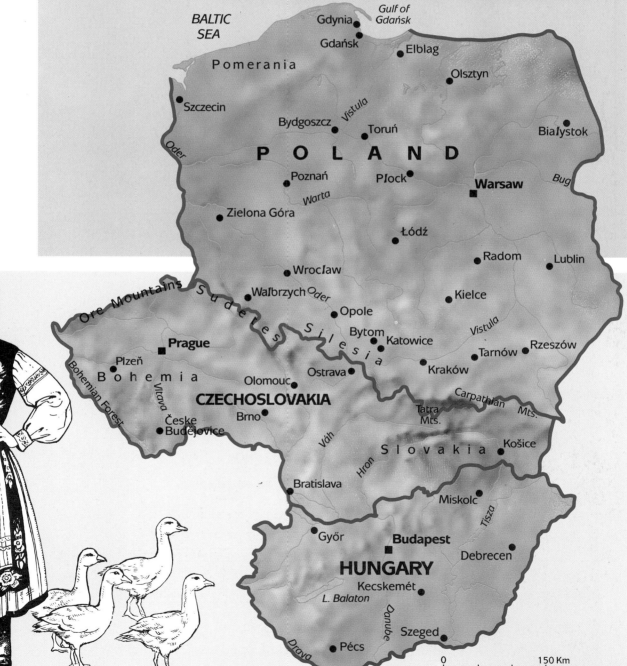

BALTIC SEA

Gulf of Gdańsk

Gdynia
Gdańsk
Elblag
Olsztyn

Pomerania

Szczecin

Vistula

Bydgoszcz
Toruń

Białystok

Oder

P O L A N D

Poznań
Płock
Warsaw

Bug

Warta

Zielona Góra

Łódź

Radom
Lublin

Wrocław

Walbrzych *Oder*

Kielce

Ore Mountains

Sudetes

Opole

Bytom
Katowice

Silesia

Vistula

Tarnów
Rzeszów

Prague

Plzeň

Bohemian Forest

B o h e m i a

Olomouc

Ostrava

Kraków

Vltava

CZECHOSLOVAKIA

Brno

Carpathian

Mts.

Tatra
Mts.

Česke
Budějovice

Váh

Hron

S l o v a k i a

Košice

Bratislava

Miskolc

Tisza

Győr

Budapest

Debrecen

HUNGARY

Kecskemét

L. Balaton

Danube

Szeged

Drava

Pécs

| 0 | | 150 Km |
| 0 | | 100 Miles |

79

FORMER SOVIET UNION

In December of 1991 the Union of Soviet Socialist Republics (U.S.S.R.) ceased to exist as a single country. Formed after the Russian Revolution of 1917, it was made up of 15 separate republics. These have now become independent countries, 11 of which agreed to form the Commonwealth of Independent States.

Russia, the largest new country, is also the largest country in the world, stretching across the globe from Europe in the west to the Pacific Ocean in the east. The Ural Mountains, running north to south, divide the country into a European part and an Asian part. Thirty-eight national minorities make up about 20 percent of the non-Russian population of the area that was the U.S.S.R.

cont. page 82.

Christians attend a Russian Orthodox service in Moscow.

Kyrgyz horseman
A lone rider nears the lake called Issyk-Kul in Kyrgyzstan. This mountainous central Asian republic borders China. Horse-breeding is an important part of the local economy. Horses are still used both by Kyrgyz shepherds high in the mountain pastures and cattle farmers in the valleys. Like many of the former Soviet republics, Kyrgyzstan's population is made up of a number of different peoples. The Kyrgyz people themselves, who are Turkic in origin, form less than half the total.

0   800 Kms
0   500 Miles

East Cape

Bering Str.

Wrangel I.

Franz Josef Land

ARCTIC   OCEAN

Severnaya Zemlya

EAST SIBERIAN SEA

New Siberian Is.

LAPTEV SEA

Chukot Range

Anadyr'

Koryak Range

Novaya Zemlya

KARA SEA

Taymyr Peninsula

Indigirka

Kolyma Range

BERING SEA

Cherskiy Range

Magadan

Kamchatka Peninsula

Yamal Peninsula

Gyda Peninsula

Verkhoyansk Range

Petropavlovsk–Kamchatskiy

Vorkuta

Kotuy

Lena

SEA OF OKHOTSK

S   i   b   e   r   i   a

Yakutsk

FEDERATION

Lower Tunguska

Ob

Upper Tunguska

Lena

Sakhalin

Yenisey

Stanovoy Range

Kuril Islands

Sovetskaya Gavan

Omsk

Tomsk

Novosibirsk

Krasnoyarsk

Angara

Lake Baykal

Yablonovy Range

Amur

Khabarovsk

Pavlodar

Novokuznetsk

Eastern Sayan

Chita

Shilka

Irtysh

Western   Sayan

Irkutsk

Ulan-Ude

L. Zaysan

Animals
This vast region is home to a huge variety of animals from the cold-loving Arctic fox to the desert monitor which lives in the central Asian deserts.

1. LONG-EARED HEDGEHOG
2. MARBLED POLECAT
3. DESERT MONITOR
4. SABLE

Vladivostok

a-Ata

Winter in the northern city of St. Petersburg is long and cold.

The European countries are the most densely populated and contain well-developed heavy industries, such as coalmining and steel manufacturing. The steel provides raw material for the manufacturing industries around Moscow and the shipbuilding industry in St. Petersburg. In the southern republics, agriculture is more dominant. Ukraine and Kazakhstan contain major grain-growing areas. However, massive amounts of food still have to be imported in order to feed their populations.

Russia's vast eastern region is sparsely populated, but has valuable resources of gas, coal, and oil. However, the inhospitable terrain makes these resources difficult to tap. Another important energy resource is hydroelectric power from the Volga River. This river, the longest in Europe, provides transportation for both people and materials. The Trans-Siberian Railway, which connects Moscow with the Pacific coast many thousands of miles to the east, is also a vital communication link.

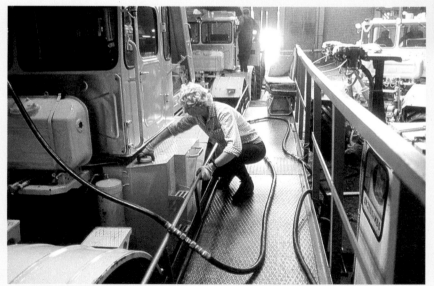

The Moscow Metro
The Moscow Metro is the most elegant subway system in the world. There are 123 subway stations, all beautifully designed and decorated.

There is no graffiti and the stations and trains are spotlessly clean, despite the 10 million people traveling along the 125 miles of track each day.

Heavy industries
Manufacturing plants, like this factory which makes trucks and tractors, are located in the major industrial regions in the west of what was once the U.S.S.R. The heavy industries produce one fifth of the world's total industrial output. Raw materials are abundant: the former U.S.S.R. had half the world's iron ore reserves and produced more steel than any other country. Since large areas of arid land have now been irrigated, making it possible to grow extra crops, there is a great demand for agricultural machinery.

FORMER SOVIET REPUBLICS

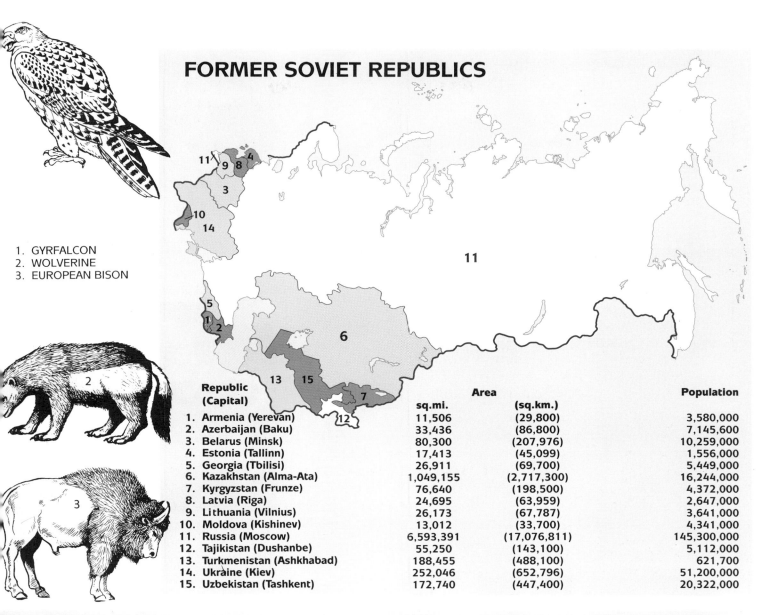

1. GYRFALCON
2. WOLVERINE
3. EUROPEAN BISON

Republic (Capital)	Area		Population
	sq. mi.	(sq. km.)	
1. Armenia (Yerevan)	11,506	(29,800)	3,580,000
2. Azerbaijan (Baku)	33,436	(86,800)	7,145,600
3. Belarus (Minsk)	80,300	(207,976)	10,259,000
4. Estonia (Tallinn)	17,413	(45,099)	1,556,000
5. Georgia (Tbilisi)	26,911	(69,700)	5,449,000
6. Kazakhstan (Alma-Ata)	1,049,155	(2,717,300)	16,244,000
7. Kyrgyzstan (Frunze)	76,640	(198,500)	4,372,000
8. Latvia (Riga)	24,695	(63,959)	2,647,000
9. Lithuania (Vilnius)	26,173	(67,787)	3,641,000
10. Moldova (Kishinev)	13,012	(33,700)	4,341,000
11. Russia (Moscow)	6,593,391	(17,076,811)	145,300,000
12. Tajikistan (Dushanbe)	55,250	(143,100)	5,112,000
13. Turkmenistan (Ashkhabad)	188,455	(488,100)	621,700
14. Ukraine (Kiev)	252,046	(652,796)	51,200,000
15. Uzbekistan (Tashkent)	172,740	(447,400)	20,322,000

Russian ballet

Members of the Bolshoi Ballet performing *Giselle.* Russian ballet is world famous and steeped in tradition. Some of the world's greatest ballets have come from Russia including works such as *Swan Lake*, *The Nutcracker,* and *Sleeping Beauty*. The country has also produced some of the world's best dancers, such as Anna Pavlova and Rudolf Nureyev. Both the Bolshoi, based in Moscow, and the St. Petersburg Ballet are among the world's best companies.

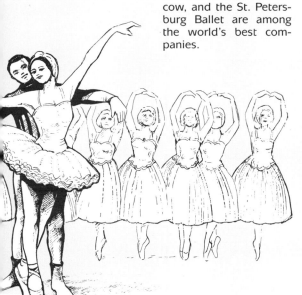

Shopping in a bazaar

Shopping scenes like this bazaar are a common sight in the new Central Asian republics. Open bazaars sell all kinds of items from bowls and baskets to lamps and rugs.

People also shop in open markets where surplus homegrown produce is sold. These are very popular; the food is fresher, though the price is often higher than in the shops.

As the old Soviet economy collapsed, supplies of food became erratic — commodities in abundance one day became scarce on other occasions, sometimes for long periods.

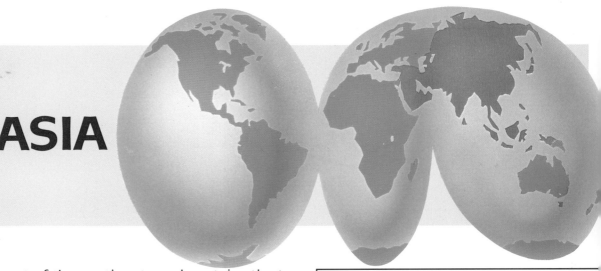

ASIA

Asia is the largest of the continents and contains the two most populous countries in the world: China and India. In contrast, many of the 14,000 islands that make up Indonesia are sparsely populated or uninhabited.

The variety of landscape is huge. In northern Russia lies a vast area of *taiga* (coniferous forest), while the desert lands of the Gobi cover much of Mongolia. Farther south lie China's vast cultivated plains, and on the edge of the Pacific Ocean volcanic islands support lush tropical vegetation.

North of the Indian subcontinent, in Nepal and Tibet, the Himalayas and the high Tibetan Plateau form the "rooftop of the world." From these icy heights flow the tributaries of some of the great river systems of this region, the Yangtze, Irrawaddy, Mekong, Ganges, and Indus rivers.

A high mountain peak in the Himalayas, in Nepal

Asia
Highest point Mount Everest (Nepal/China) 29,028ft. (8848m.)
Lowest point Shore of Dead Sea (Israel/Jordan) 1310ft. (399m.) below sea level
Longest river Yangtze (China) 3915mi. (6300km.)
Largest lake Caspian Sea 143,630sq.mi. (372,000sq.km.)

INDIA
Official name Bharat
Area 1,269,350 sq. miles (3,287,590 sq. km.)
Population 853,400,000
Capital New Delhi (pop. Delhi 6,220,000)
Largest cities Calcutta (9,166,000) Bombay (8,202,000) Madras (4,277,000) Bangalore (2,914,000)
Currency Indian Rupee
Official language(s) Hindi and English (14 regional languages are also spoken)
Chief products Rice, wheat, sugarcane, jute, cotton, tea, coal, chemicals, fertilizers, vehicles
Exports Textiles, jewelry, clothing, leather goods, iron ore, tea, fish
Imports Crude oil, iron and steel, precious stones

MALDIVES
Area 115 sq. miles (298 sq. km.)
Population 200,000
Capital Malé

CHINA (PEOPLE'S REPUBLIC OF CHINA)
Official name Zhonghua Renmin Gonghe-guo
Area 3,695,500 sq. miles (9,571,300 sq. km.)
Population 1,072,330,000
Capital Beijing (Peking) (pop. 5,970,000)
Currency Yuan
Official language(s) Mandarin (also Cantonese and other dialects)
Chief products Coal, iron, steel, machinery, textiles, chemicals, oil, tin, minerals, rice, tea, silkworms, pulses
Exports Livestock, textiles, ore, metals, tea, clothing
Imports Vehicles, machinery, chemicals

HONG KONG (U.K.)
Area 412 sq. mi. (1067 sq. km.)
Population 5,533,000
MACAO (PORTUGAL)
Area 6 sq. mi. (16 sq. km.)
Population 392,000

JAPAN
Official name Nihon
Area 145,875 sq. miles (377,815 sq. km.)
Population 123,600,000
Capital Tokyo (pop. 8,155,781)
Currency Yen
Official language(s) Japanese
Chief products Vehicles, machinery, electrical goods, iron, steel, chemicals, textiles, fish, rice
Exports Steel, vehicles, electrical equipment, ships
Imports Minerals, crude oil, raw materials, food

SRI LANKA
Area 24,886 sq. miles (64,453 sq. km.)
Population 17,200,000
Capital Colombo
Chief products Graphite, minerals, precious stones

INDONESIA
Area 735,358 sq. miles (1,904,569 sq. km.)
Population 189,400,000
Capital Jakarta
Official language(s) Bahasa and Indonesian
Chief products Copra, spices, palm oil, sugar, rubber, tea, coffee, tobacco, rice, oil, lumber, minerals

BHUTAN
Area 18,147 sq. miles (47,000 sq. km.)
Population 1,447,000
Capital Thimphu

BRUNEI
Area 2226 sq. miles (5765 sq. km.)
Population 226,000
Capital Bandar Seri Begawan

PAKISTAN
Official name Islami Jamhuriya-e-Pakistan
Area 310,403 sq. miles (803,943 sq. km.)
Population 114,600,000
Capital Islamabad
Official language(s) Urdu
Chief products Cotton, rice, wheat, sugarcane, corn, tobacco, salt, leather, wool, fertilizers, paints, carpets, paper

SINGAPORE
Area 238 sq. miles (616 sq. km.)
Population 2,647,100
Chief products Oil refining, chemicals, ships, electrical equipment, paper, machinery, textiles

NEPAL
Area 56,827 sq. miles
(147,181 sq. km.)
Population 17,632,960
Capital Kathmandu
Chief products Cattle,
corn, rice, oilseeds, wheat

MONGOLIA
Area 604,250 sq. miles
(1,565,000 sq. km.)
Population 1,900,000
Capital Ulan Bator
Chief products Livestock,
wool, hides and skins,
minerals

NORTH KOREA
Area 7929 sq. miles
(120,538 sq. km.)
Population 21,390,000
Capital Pyongyang
Chief products Chemicals,
iron and steel, rice, corn,
machinery, wheat

SOUTH KOREA
Area 38,310 sq. miles
(99,222 sq. km.)
Population 42,082,128
Capital Seoul
Chief products Chemicals,
textiles, iron and steel, rice,
electrical equipment

BANGLADESH
Area 55,598 sq. miles
(143,998 sq. km.)
Population 102,563,000
Capital Dhaka
Chief products Jute,
paper, textiles, natural gas,
leather, rice, sugarcane

MYANMAR (BURMA)
Area 261,218 sq. miles
(672,552 sq. km.)
Population 46,300,000
Capital Yangon (Rangoon)
Chief products Silk, tin,
lumber, copper, rubber

THAILAND
Area 198,115 sq. miles
(513,115 sq. km.)
Population 54,536,000
Capital Bangkok
Chief products Teak,
bamboo, fish, tin, iron ore,
natural gas, rice, rubber

LAOS
Area 91,400 sq. miles
(236,800 sq. km.)
Population 4,218,000
Capital Vientiane
Chief products Cattle,
citrus fruits, coffee, opium,
cotton, teak, rice, salt

CAMBODIA
Area 69,898 sq. miles
(181,035 sq. km.)
Population 7,688,000
Capital Phnom Penh
Chief products Cement,
paper, textiles, cattle, rice

VIETNAM
Area 127,246 sq. miles
(328,566 sq. km.)
Population 70,200,000
Capital Hanoi
Chief products Cement,
iron and steel, paper, coal,
textiles, rice

KAZAKHSTAN
Area 1,049,155 sq. miles
(2,717,300 sq. km.)
Population 16,690,300
Capital Alma-Ata
Chief products Grain,
cotton, fruit, coal,
petroleum, electric power

KYRGYZSTAN
Area 76,640 sq. miles
(198,500 sq. km.)
Population 4,372,000
Capital Bishkek
Chief products Grain,
vegetables, coal, petroleum,
cement, steel

TAJIKISTAN
Area 55,250 sq. miles
(143,100 sq. km.)
Population 5,112,000
Capital Dushanbe
Chief products Cotton,
vegetables, grain, coal,
petroleum, natural gas

PHILIPPINES
Area 115,831 sq. miles
(300,000 sq. km.)
Population 56,004,000
Capital Manila
Chief products Fish,
pineapples, rice, metals, oil
products, mother of pearl,
mahogany, textiles

UZBEKISTAN
Area 172,740 sq. miles
(447,400 sq. km.)
Population 20,322,000
Capital Tashkent
Chief products Cotton,
vegetables, grain, paper
products, plastics

BHUTAN

BRUNEI

MALDIVES

TAIWAN
Area 13,890 sq. miles
(35,590 sq. km.)
Population 20,200,000
Capital Taipei

MALAYSIA
Area 127,320 sq. miles
(329,758 sq. km.)
Population 17,900,000
Capital Kuala Lumpur
Chief products Rubber,
rice, cacao, coconuts,
minerals, palm oil, pepper

TURKMENISTAN
Area 188,455 sq. miles
(488,100 sq. km.)
Population 3,621,700
Capital Ashkhabad
Chief products Cotton,
vegetables, grain,
petroleum, fertilizers

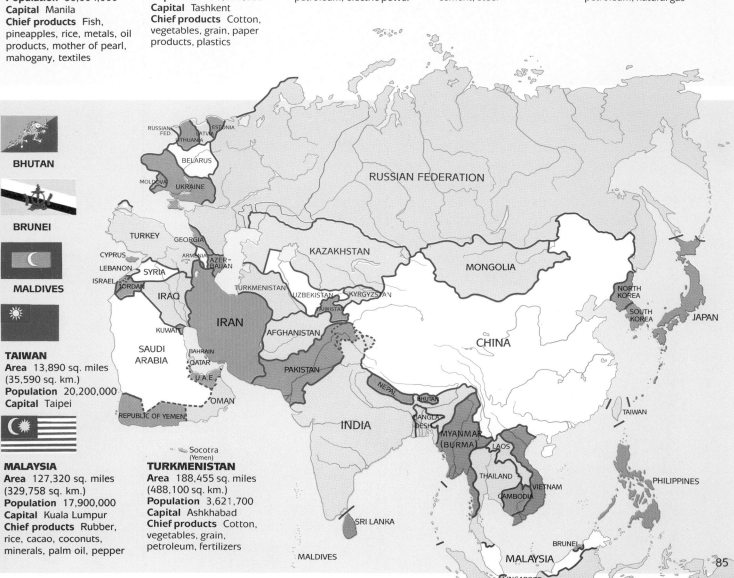

The Middle East is the name given to that part of south-west Asia which lies between the Mediterranean and the Indian subcontinent. Its geographical position has led to a mix of peoples and cultures from both East and West. A series of mountain ranges runs across the north of the region from the Taurus Mountains in Turkey to the Hindu Kush, the western foothills of the Himalayas, in Afghanistan.

The climate along the Mediterranean coast is temperate but farther south the Arabian peninsula and central Iran are sparsely populated desert lands. The "empty quarter" in Saudi Arabia is uninhabited except for a small number of nomadic Bedouin. Most of the population lives in the coastal regions next to the Red Sea, the Gulf, and the Indian Ocean. Oil exploitation, shipping, and some agriculture enable coastal communities to thrive.

Sunset over Jerusalem with the Islamic shrine, Dome of the Rock in the background.
(top) Nomadic huts or *yurts* in the Hindu Kush regions of Afghanistan.

IRAN
Official name Jomhori-e-Islami-e-Irân
Area 636,296 sq. miles (1,648,000 sq. km.)
Population 49,857,384
Capital Tehran (pop. 6,022,029)
Largest cities Mashhad (1,500,000)
Esfahan (1,000,000)
Tabriz (852,296)
Shiraz (800,416)
Bakhtaran (531,350)
Currency Iranian Rial
Official language(s) Farsi (Persian) (Turkish, Kurdish and Arabic are also spoken)
Chief products Oil, natural gas, iron ore, coal, zinc and lead, sugar, textiles, cement, wheat, rice, sugar beet, tobacco, fish, cotton, steel, oilseeds, wool
Exports Oil, gas, carpets, fruit, caviar, textiles, cement
Imports Livestock, minerals, chemicals, iron and steel, machinery, vehicles

ISRAEL
Official name Medinat Israel
Area 8473 sq. miles (21,946 sq. km.)
Population 4,406,500
Capital Jerusalem (pop. 428,668)
Largest cities Tel-Aviv - Yafo (327,625)
Haifa (235,775)
Currency New Shekel
Official language(s) Hebrew and Arabic
Chief products Citrus fruits (especially oranges), olives, rice, vegetables, tobacco, wheat, barley, corn, sesame, chemicals, clothing, finished diamonds, machinery, salts, phosphates
Exports Citrus fruits (oranges), vegetables, finished diamonds, pearls, manufactured goods
Imports Rough diamonds, electrical equipment, iron and steel, chemicals, crude oil, cereals, vehicles

SAUDI ARABIA
Official name Al-Mamlaka al-Arabiya as-Sa'udiya
Area 926,745 sq. miles (2,400,900 sq. km.)
Population 13,612,000
Capital Riyadh (pop. 666,840)
Largest cities Jiddah (Administrative capital) (561,104)
Mecca (366,801)
Ta'if (204,857)
Medina (198,186)
Dammam (127,844)
Hofuf (101,271)
Currency Saudi Riyal
Official language(s) Arabic
Chief products Oil, cement, fertilizers, steel, petrochemicals, camels, citrus fruits, dates, goats, rice, vegetables, wheat
Exports Crude and refined oil
Imports Food, tobacco, metals and metal products, precision tools, precious stones and metals, ceramics, glass

TURKEY
Official name Türkiye Cumhuriyeti
Area 300,948 sq. miles (779,452 sq. km.)
Population 56,700,000
Capital Ankara (pop. 2,235,035)
Largest cities Istanbul (5,475,982)
Izmir (1,489,772)
Adana (777,554)
Bursa (612,510)
Currency Turkish Lira
Official language(s) Turkish (Kurdish is also spoken)
Chief products Iron and steel, fertilizers, machinery, vehicles, processed food and drink, paper products, textiles, barley, corn, cotton, fruit, wheat
Exports Agricultural products, textiles, tobacco, citrus fruits, figs, olives, salt, hazelnuts
Imports Machinery, iron and steel, oil, medicines, dyes, vehicles

SYRIA

Official name Al-Jumhuriya al-Arabiya as-Souriya
Area 71,498 sq. miles (185,180 sq. km.)
Population 10,612,000
Capital Damascus
Official language(s) Arabic
Chief products Oil, natural gas, phosphates, asphalt, iron ore, tobacco, oil products, cotton

LEBANON

Official name Al-Jumhuriya al-Lubnaniya
Area 4036 sq. miles (10,452 sq. km.)
Population 2,762,000
Capital Beirut
Official language(s) Arabic (French is also spoken)
Chief products Cement, chemicals, electrical equipment, furniture, textiles, citrus fruits

JORDAN

Official name Al-Mamlaka al-Urduniya al-Hashemiyah
Area 37,738 sq. miles (97,740 sq. km.)
Population 4,100,000
Capital Amman
Official language(s) Arabic
Chief products Barley, fruit, olives, goats, lentils, sheep, vegetables, wheat, phosphates

IRAQ

Official name Al-Jumhuriya al-'Iraqiya
Area 169,235 sq. miles (438,317 sq. km.)
Population 16,110,000
Capital Baghdad
Official language(s) Arabic (Kurdish is also spoken)
Chief products Oil, dates, fruit, wheat, barley, rice, millet, cotton, tobacco, livestock, leather products

AFGHANISTAN

Official name Da Jamhuriat Afghanistan
Area 251,773 sq. miles (652,225 sq. km.)
Population 15,900,000
Capital Kabul
Official language(s) Pashtu, Dari
Chief products Cement, textiles, rugs, coal, gold, natural gas, corn, cotton, nuts, rice, sheep

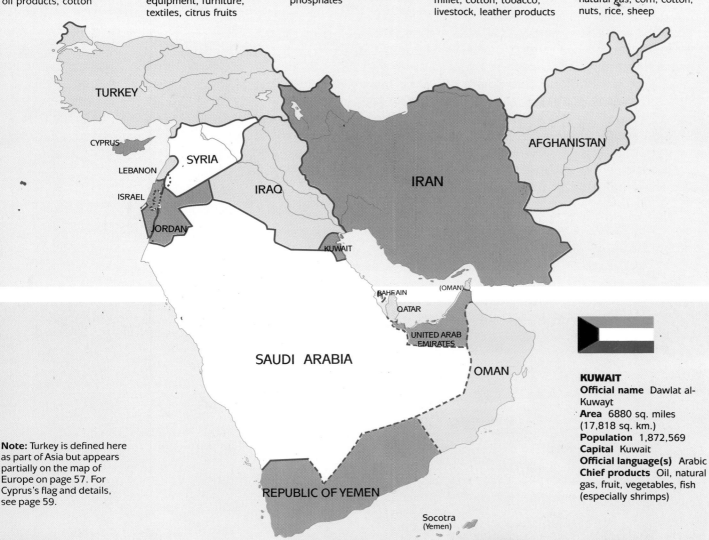

Note: Turkey is defined here as part of Asia but appears partially on the map of Europe on page 57. For Cyprus's flag and details, see page 59.

KUWAIT

Official name Dawlat al-Kuwayt
Area 6880 sq. miles (17,818 sq. km.)
Population 1,872,569
Capital Kuwait
Official language(s) Arabic
Chief products Oil, natural gas, fruit, vegetables, fish (especially shrimps)

YEMEN

Official name Al-Jumhuriya al-Yemeniya
Area 184,345 sq. miles (477,530 sq. km.)
Population 11,494,353
Capital San'a
Official language(s) Arabic
Chief products Sorghum, sesame, dyes, fish, refined oil, coffee, khat, fruit, barley, cotton, dates, vegetables

OMAN

Official name Saltanat Uman
Area 104,970 sq. miles (271,950 sq. km.)
Population 1,334,000 (estimate)
Capital Muscat
Official language(s) Arabic (English is also spoken)
Chief products Oil, coconuts, dates, limes, livestock, sugarcane

UNITED ARAB EMIRATES

Official name Al-Imarat al-Arabiya al-Muttahida
Area 29,010 sq. miles (75,150 sq. km.)
Population 11,384,000
Capital Abu Dhabi
Official language(s) Arabic
Chief products Oil, fish (especially shrimps), dates

QATAR

Official name Dawlat Qatar
Area 4416 sq. miles (11,437 sq. km.)
Population 369,079
Capital Doha
Official language(s) Arabic (English is also spoken)
Chief products Oil and oil products

BAHRAIN

Official name Dawlat al-Bahrayn
Area 266.9 sq. miles (691.2 sq. km.)
Population 412,000
Capital Manama
Official language(s) Arabic (English is also spoken)
Chief products Oil, aluminum, boats, building materials, oil products, plastics, grains

TURKEY AND NEAR EAST

Turkey and the Near East (which includes the countries of Syria, Jordan, Lebanon, and Israel) lie at the eastern end of the Mediterranean and extend south to the deserts of Saudi Arabia. People of three main religions — Islam, Judaism, and Christianity — inhabit this region and all regard Jerusalem as their holy city. Religious differences are the cause of much conflict in the Near East. In 1948 the state of Israel was created in part of what had been the British Mandate of Palestine. The existence of the Jewish state has been contested by its Arab neighbors ever since.

Much of Turkey and the coastal regions of Syria, Lebanon, and Israel have a warm Mediterranean climate. Here the staple foods of wheat and barley are grown, as well as export crops such as tobacco, cotton, hazelnuts, citrus fruits, figs, and olives. Farther east the land is hot, dry desert where agriculture is impossible without irrigation. The Dead Sea, the lowest point on the Earth, is mined for its rich salt deposits.

The "Cotton Castle" Many tourists visit Turkey for its unspoiled beauty. These scenic chalk terraces lie inland, near Denizli. In Turkish their name is *Pamukkale* which means "Cotton Castle." Tourists come here to bathe in the spring water, which comes out of the ground at temperatures of up to 95 degrees Fahrenheit.

A cotton factory in Syria
Cotton is grown extensively on the cultivated steppe lands of northeast Syria, the major agricultural region around the Euphrates and Asi rivers. This textile factory in Damascus is one of many which produces material for export. Best known is the heavy, patterned fabric *damask* which takes its name from the city.

Israel — land of the Jews
At their prayers many observant Jews wear *tefillin*, small boxes containing Hebrew scriptures that remind them to live by the Law of God.

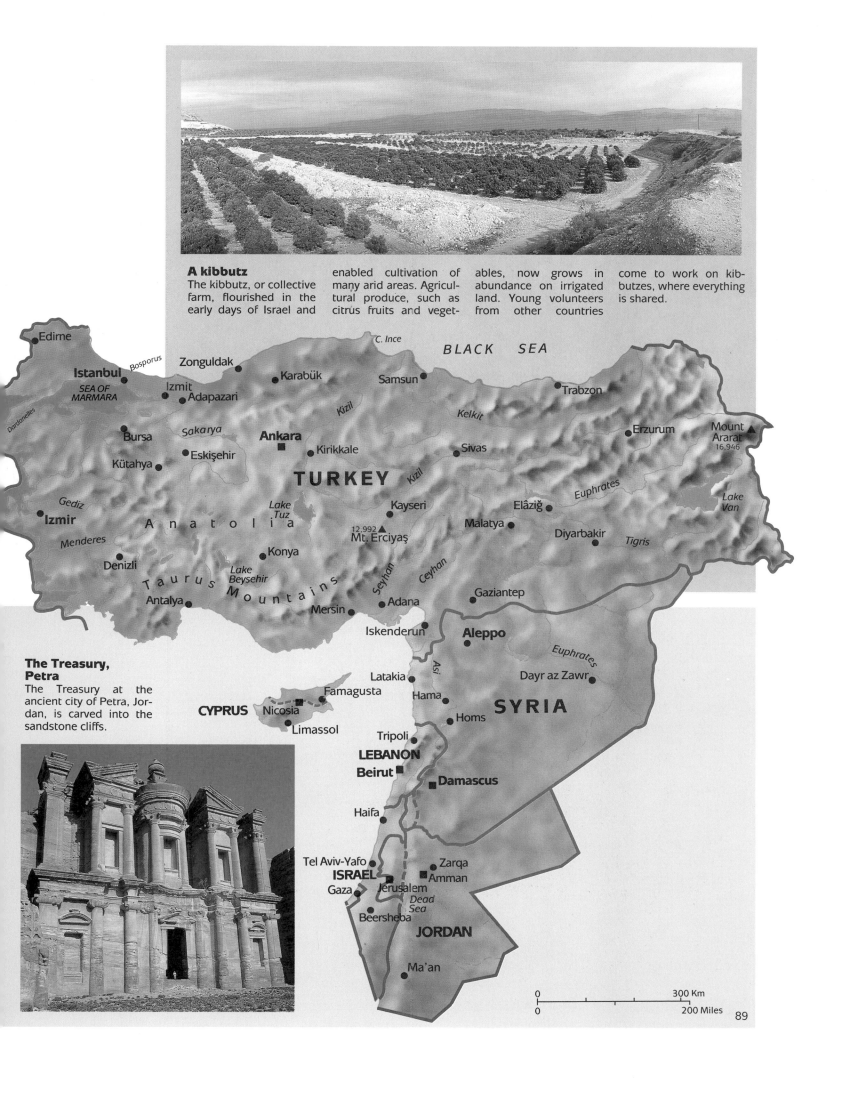

A kibbutz
The kibbutz, or collective farm, flourished in the early days of Israel and enabled cultivation of many arid areas. Agricultural produce, such as citrus fruits and vegetables, now grows in abundance on irrigated land. Young volunteers from other countries come to work on kibbutzes, where everything is shared.

The Treasury, Petra
The Treasury at the ancient city of Petra, Jordan, is carved into the sandstone cliffs.

BLACK SEA

Edirne
Istanbul
Bosporus
Zonguldak
Karabük
Samsun
Trabzon
Dardanelles
SEA OF MARMARA
Izmit
Adapazari
Kizil
Kelkit
Erzurum
Mount Ararat 16,946
Bursa
Sakarya
Ankara
Kirikkale
Sivas
C. Ince
Kütahya
Eskişehir
TURKEY
Kizil
Euphrates
Lake Van
Izmir
Gediz
A n a t o l i a
Lake Tuz
Kayseri
Eläzığ
Malatya
Diyarbakir
Tigris
Menderes
12,992 ▲ Mt. Erciyaş
Konya
Denizli
Lake Beyşehir
T a u r u s   M o u n t a i n s
Seyhan
Ceyhan
Antalya
Mersin
Adana
Gaziantep
Iskenderun
Aleppo
Euphrates
Latakia
Asi
Dayr az Zawr
Hama
SYRIA
CYPRUS
Nicosia
Famagusta
Homs
Limassol
Tripoli
LEBANON
Beirut
Damascus
Haifa
Tel Aviv-Yafo
Zarqa
ISRAEL
Amman
Gaza
Jerusalem
Dead Sea
Beersheba
JORDAN
Ma'an

0 — 300 Km
0 — 200 Miles

89

ARABIAN PENINSULA

In common with all the Middle Eastern countries except Israel, the Arabian peninsula nations are mostly Islamic. The holiest of the Muslim cities, Mecca, is in Saudi Arabia. The people of this region are Arabs and they all speak a common language: Arabic.

The Arabian peninsula is a hot, dry land which is very largely desert. The only large area with enough rain to grow crops is in the highlands of Yemen. Otherwise, some farming is possible in desert "oases," and other small areas where underground water is used to irrigate crops. The date palm is a common sight in such areas.

All the countries of the Arabian peninsula, except Yemen, have discovered large reserves of oil in recent times. Oil is pumped from underground into ships which export it to Europe, North America, Asia, and Africa. The money from selling oil has made these countries very rich. Many new roads and buildings have been constructed, and some Arabs no longer ride camels as before but drive expensive cars.

Arabian desert
Parts of the desert are covered by shifting sand dunes. Some of these areas are so large they are known as "sand seas," or *ergs* in Arabic. The *erg* of *Rub'al Khali*, or the "Empty Quarter," in Saudi Arabia is about the size of Georgia in the United States.

A market, Yemen
At a market, or *souk*, in a town in Yemen a man weighs homemade sugared cakes before selling them. These cakes are a favorite delicacy. In many of the markets of Yemen each street has its own specialty — hats, sandals, medicinal potions, herbs, cloth, and pottery are all laid out and bartered for. Shoppers fill their turbans with the day's purchases.

Oil in the Arabian peninsula

The photograph above, shows a Saudi Arabian oil refinery. Oil is the most important natural resource in the countries of the Arabian peninsula, especially those around the Persian Gulf such as Kuwait, Saudi Arabia, Qatar, and the United Arab Emirates. In some parts the oil is found beneath the sea; in other areas it is beneath the desert. Once it has been extracted, most of the oil has to be transported to other countries. Oil found in southern Oman, for example, is pumped through a pipeline 280 miles to the north coast where it is loaded onto ships. The countries that import oil use it to make gasoline, fuel oil, chemicals, and plastics.

Saudi Arabia exports more oil than any other country in the world. Japan and the U.S.A. are its main customers. The money Saudi Arabia earns from oil is used to buy all sorts of machinery and manufactured goods, and many of these are bought from Japan and the U.S.A.. Much of the money is also spent on building things: new roads, houses, offices, airports, and mosques. Saudi Arabia also buys much of its food from abroad since the people cannot grow enough of their own in the harsh climate. Saudi Arabia does not import any alcohol or any foods with pork in them. This is because the Islamic religion does not allow Muslims to eat pork or drink alcohol.

Mosque

The photograph shows a mosque in Abu Dhabi, in the United Arab Emirates. The mosque is the Muslim place of worship. Like churches in Christian countries, mosques are often very fine buildings, some many hundreds of years old. The most important mosques have several domes and a minaret, or tower. It is from the minaret that the *muezzin*, a mosque official, will call worshippers to prayer five times a day. Most of the inhabitants of the Arabian countries are Muslims, followers of Islam. This religion teaches that there is one God, Allah, and that Muhammad was his prophet. The Koran is the sacred book of Islam.

SOUTHWEST ASIA

Between Mesopotamia and the Himalayas lie the countries of Iraq, Iran, and Afghanistan. Afghanistan is a poor country. Since 1979, civil war has ravaged the country. Many people are nomadic herders, constantly moving their animals to new grazing lands.

Iran and Iraq have become rich by exploiting their resources of oil and gas. Most of the oil is exported by tanker through the Persian Gulf, to Japan, the U.S.A. and Western Europe. Although Iran and Iraq are neighbors, religious differences and disputed territories led to war from 1980 to 1988. The Iraqis are Arabic, Sunni Muslims whereas the Iranians are descended from Asian peoples, speak Farsi, and are Shiite Muslims. Iraq invaded Kuwait in 1990, leading to the outbreak of war in January 1991. Allied forces from the U.S., Saudi Arabia, Britain, France and over twenty other nations defeated the Iraquis in February 1991.

Persian carpets
The ancient tradition of carpetmaking continues today in Iran. The carpets produced are better known as Persian rugs, and are prized as possessions worldwide. The rugs are worked by hand in silk or wool, using twine dyed in vivid colors and woven into intricate patterns. They are then washed and draped over rocks to dry in the sun.

The Marsh Arabs
The marshlands of southern central Iraq, around the Tigris and Euphrates rivers, are inhabited by the Marsh Arabs. The area is relatively inaccessible and as a result the Marsh Arabs' traditional way of life has remained almost untouched by outside influences. Many people still live in reed houses built on piles of rushes in up to six feet of water. Transport is by elegant canoes.

Band-i-Amir Lake
Much of Afghanistan is desolate and bleak countryside which supports little or no vegetation. A high, inhospitable region called the Hindu Kush runs across the northeast of the country to meet the massive Himalayan mountain range. Band-i-Amir lake (*in the picture*) is situated in an area known as Koh-i-Baba, northwest of Kabul. It is a natural reservoir, formed by the slow buildup of mineral deposits which have trapped the water. Irrigation ditches have been dug, and some members of the traditionally nomadic Kuchi tribe have settled on land given by the government. Others move through these remote mountain areas in search of pastureland.

Persepolis, southern Iran

The ruins of the great palace of Persepolis as they stand today in southern Iran. Building work was started on the palace in 520 BC under the order of Darius the First, ruler of the Persian Empire which covered much of modern Iran, Iraq, Afghanistan, and the Near East. Darius and his court used Persepolis only once a year, at New Year, when tribute was brought to him by the various peoples of his vast Empire. Some of these tribute bearers are depicted on the great staircase in the foreground of this picture.

Praying to Mecca

Every aspect of a Muslim's life is guided by the principles of Islam, and all Muslim men are required to pray five times each day. At the mosque every worshipper has his own mat on which he kneels, praying in the direction of Mecca, the birthplace of Muhammad.

Friday is the holy day for Muslims; all work is forbidden, and special prayers are conducted. The Koran, the holy book of Islam, records the preaching of Muhammad and lays down laws by which Muslims must live.

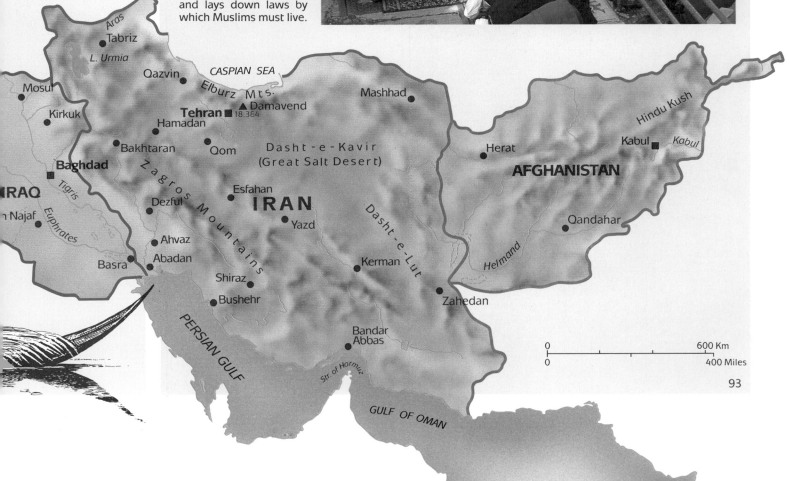

Aras
Tabriz
L. Urmia
Mosul
Kirkuk
Qazvin
CASPIAN SEA
Elburz Mts.
Mashhad
Tehran ■ 18,384 ▲ Damavend
Hindu Kush
Hamadan
Bakhtaran
Qom
Kabul ■ Kabul
Baghdad
Zagros
Dasht-e-Kavir
(Great Salt Desert)
Herat
AFGHANISTAN
IRAQ
Tigris
Esfahan
Dezful
IRAN
Yazd
Dasht-e-Lut
Qandahar
n Najaf
Euphrates
Ahvaz
Mountains
Basra
Abadan
Helmand
Kerman
Shiraz
Zahedan
Bushehr
PERSIAN GULF
Bandar Abbas
0   600 Km
0   400 Miles
Str of Hormuz

GULF OF OMAN

SOUTH ASIA

The region of South Asia is often called the Indian subcontinent. In the north, the high, snowclad peaks and valleys of the Himalayas are sparsely populated. Farther south hot and overcrowded cities, such as Calcutta and Bombay, are home to millions of people, many of whom live on the streets or in temporary shanty towns.

Both India and Bangladesh have huge, and growing, populations – over 800 million people live in India alone. In the past people have settled here from all over Asia, and more than 200 languages are still spoken across the region. Hinduism and Buddhism, two of the world's major religions, started in this area. Today, Pakistan and Bangladesh are mainly Muslim states and India is predominantly Hindu.

Rice, wheat, and cotton are important crops and both India and Pakistan are major textile exporters. However, much agriculture is still subsistence farming, and relies on the annual monsoon rains which fall between June and October.

Quet

PAK

Baluchistan

Central Makran Ran

Karachi

Rice growing in Pakistan

Rice is the main crop grown in the Punjab region of Pakistan. The rice fields are flooded with water taken from the River Indus. Oxen are still used for the heavy labor.

The River Ganges at Varanasi

These Hindus are bathing in the River Ganges because the waters are believed to be holy. Every year millons of pilgrims come to the sacred Indian city of Varanasi to wash away their sins.

An Indian spice seller

This man is sitting at his spice stall in an Indian bazaar. Spices are very important in Indian food – one of the most popu-lar dishes is highly spiced curry. Some of the most common spices are pep-per, ginger, mustard, and cinnamon.

For centuries India has had a flourishing spice trade with countries in the West. Before refri-geration was invented, spices were used to dis-guise the taste and smell of food that was not fresh.

94

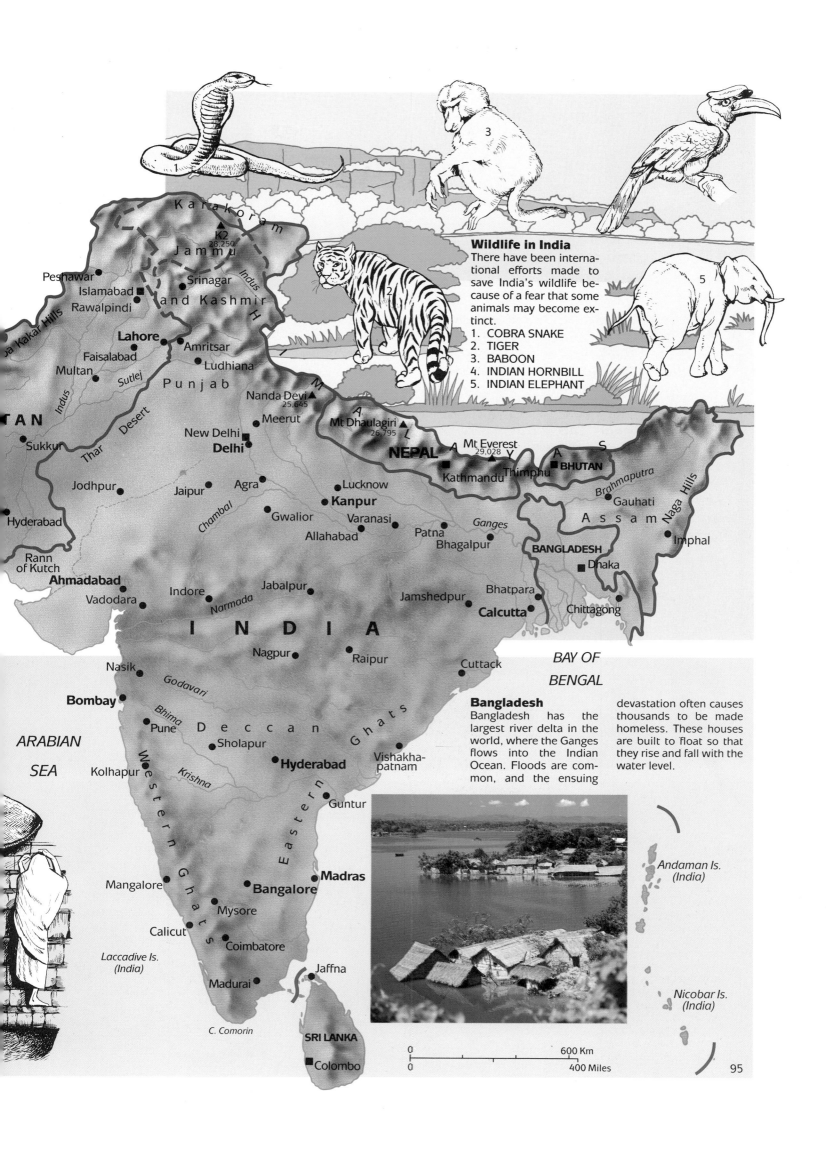

Wildlife in India

There have been international efforts made to save India's wildlife because of a fear that some animals may become extinct.
1. COBRA SNAKE
2. TIGER
3. BABOON
4. INDIAN HORNBILL
5. INDIAN ELEPHANT

Peshawar
Islamabad
Rawalpindi
a Kakar Hills
Lahore
Faisalabad
Multan
Sukkur
Jodhpur
Hyderabad
Rann of Kutch
Ahmadabad
Vadodara
Nasik
Bombay
Pune
Sholapur
Kolhapur
Mangalore
Calicut
Madurai

K2
28,250
Srinagar
and Kashmir
Amritsar
Ludhiana
Punjab
Nanda Devi
25,645
Meerut
New Delhi
Delhi
Jaipur
Agra
Gwalior
Indore
Jabalpur
Nagpur

I N D I A

K a r a k o r a m
J a m m u

Thar Desert
Sutlej
Indus
Chambal
Narmada

Kanpur
Lucknow
Varanasi
Allahabad
Patna

Mt Dhaulagiri
26,795
NEPAL
Kathmandu
Mt Everest
29,028
Thimphu **BHUTAN**

Ganges
Bhagalpur

BANGLADESH
Dhaka

Brahmaputra
Gauhati
A s s a m Naga Hills
Imphal

Bhatpara
Jamshedpur
Calcutta
Chittagong

Raipur
Cuttack

D e c c a n
Godavari
Bhima
Krishna
Hyderabad
Guntur
Vishakha-patnam

Eastern Ghats
Western Ghats

Madras
Bangalore
Mysore
Coimbatore

ARABIAN SEA

BAY OF BENGAL

Bangladesh

Bangladesh has the largest river delta in the world, where the Ganges flows into the Indian Ocean. Floods are common, and the ensuing devastation often causes thousands to be made homeless. These houses are built to float so that they rise and fall with the water level.

Laccadive Is. (India)

C. Comorin

SRI LANKA
Colombo

Andaman Is. (India)

Nicobar Is. (India)

0		600 Km
0		400 Miles

95

SOUTHEAST ASIA

The region known as Southeast Asia includes more than 20,000 islands, mostly in Indonesia and the Philippines. Indonesia is the largest archipelago in the world, spanning 3180 miles — nearly the width of the U.S.A.

The staple crop of the area is rice. Thailand, in particular, is known as the "rice bowl of Asia." Other crops include coffee, rubber, sugarcane, and coconuts. Most of the countries of this region have economies based on agriculture, and are relatively undeveloped. In contrast, Singapore is an international port and commercial center, and Brunei, a tiny kingdom on the north coast of Borneo, is rich from oil. Indonesia, too, exports oil and has a lucrative and thriving tourist industry.

Mining in Southeast Asia

Tin is mined throughout Malaysia and is a major source of income for the country.

· Mining techniques are often basic, but modern technology is being introduced. From ports such as Port Kelang vast quantities of tin and one of Malaysia's other major commodities, rubber, are exported.

Teak logging

In Thailand's northern forests, domesticated elephants move felled teak trees to the sawmills. The elephants are used for their massive strength and mobility on ground which is unsuitable for heavy machinery.

Wildlife

Two exotic examples of the wildlife of the region are shown here.
1. PROBOSCIS MONKEY
2. MALAYAN TAPIR

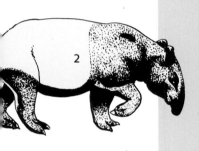

Balinese dancers

These two young Balinese dancers are performing the graceful *legong* dance wearing flower headpieces and dazzling costumes. Such dances were originally performed to please the gods during festivals, when temples throughout the island were decorated with flowers and food offerings for them. Though they still play an important part in village life, many of the traditional rituals are now more often performed for the tourists who come to enjoy this tropical paradise.

The Shwesandaw Pagoda

The Shwesandaw Pagoda, the most highly revered religious building in Myanmar (Burma), is situated on the eastern bank of the River Irrawaddy, five miles south of Pyè.

Buddhism is the main religion in this region. Every village has at least one monastery, and orange clad monks are a common sight.

Batan Is.

Babuyan Is.

Luzon

Quezon City

Manila

Mindoro

PHILIPPINES

Samar

Panay

Palawan

Cebu

Negros

SULU SEA

Mindanao

Davao

▲ Kinabalu
13,455

Sulu Arch.

Sabah

CELEBES SEA

Manado

Halmahera

Biak

Sula Is.

Sulawesi (Celebes)

Moluccas

Buru

Banjarmasin

Ceram

Jayapura

INDONESIA

Ujung Pandang

Butung

BANDA SEA

Maloke Range
▲ Puncak Jaya
16,500

Aru Is.

Irian Jaya

Semarang

Madura

FLORES SEA

Yogyakarta

Surabaya

Lesser Sunda Islands

Wetar

Tanimbar Islands

Malang

Bali

Sumbawa

Alor

Lombok

Flores

Timor

Sumba

Nang

Minh City

SOUTH CHINA SEA

Bandar Seri Begawan

BRUNEI

YSIA

Sarawak

Kuching

Borneo

Kapuas

Kalimantan

Mahakam

Barito

AVA SEA

TNAM

CHINA AND KOREA

This region covers a vast area of eastern Asia, running from the barren hills and plains of the Gobi, a vast desert in Mongolia, south to the Tibetan Plateau and east to the fertile plains and river valleys of China.

China itself is roughly the same size as the U.S.A., yet its population is more than four times as big, and it is one of the poorest countries in the world. Much of the population is concentrated in the southeast of the country, where rice and tea are cultivated, and silk is produced.

There are mineral reserves of coal, iron ore, oil, and gas, mainly in the west. Industry is developed in and around such cities as Beijing (Peking) and Shanghai, where textiles and electrical goods are manufactured for export. cont. on page 100

The Potala Palace in Tibet

The Potala Palace stands on a high mount overlooking the city of Lhasa in the Himalayan mountains. It was once the residence of the Dalai Lama who is Tibet's spiritual leader, but in 1959 he was forced to leave the country by the Chinese Communists. Lhasa is a holy city for Tibetan Buddhists who worship the statue of Buddha in the temple of the Potala Palace.

The Chinese canal scene

On the Great Plain in eastern China there are numerous canals which link up with some of the country's rivers. The canals bring water to dry districts and are used as transport routes. In this picture, two men are steering their barge with a cargo of hay through a town, the canal banks crowded with ramshackle houses.

98

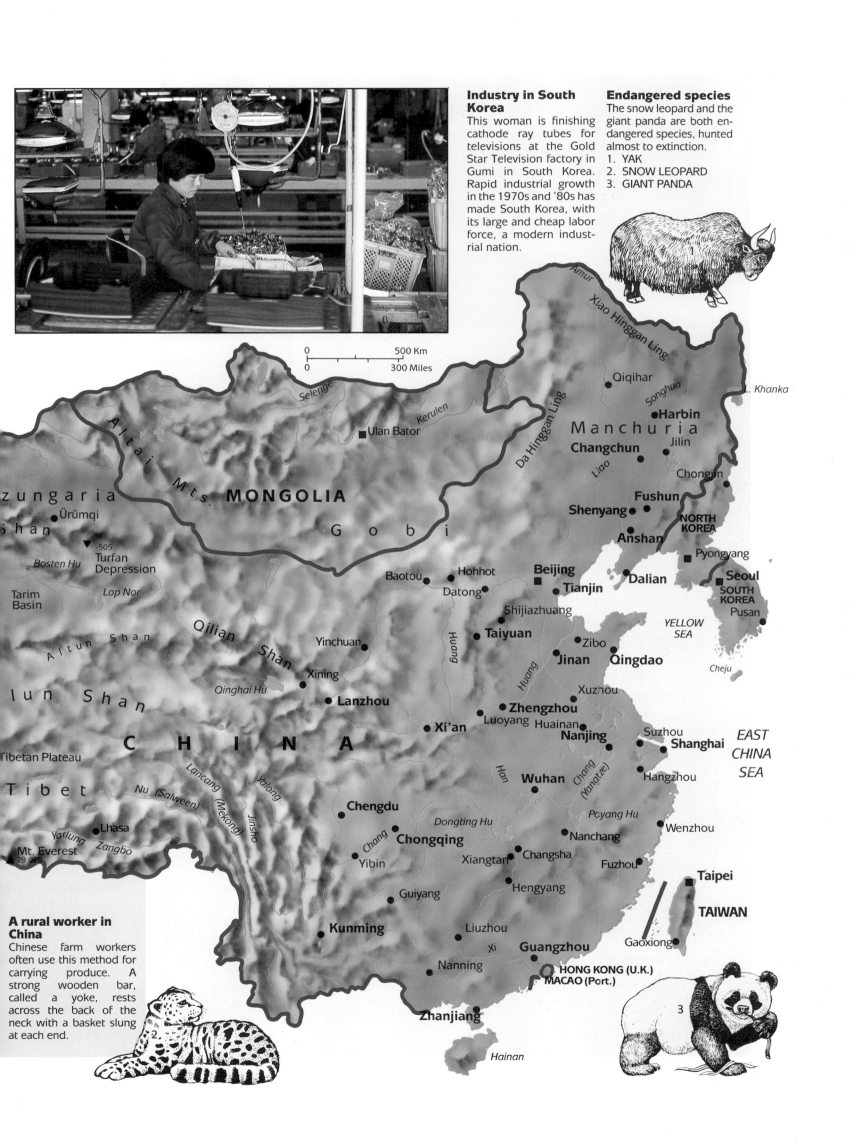

Industry in South Korea

This woman is finishing cathode ray tubes for televisions at the Gold Star Television factory in Gumi in South Korea. Rapid industrial growth in the 1970s and '80s has made South Korea, with its large and cheap labor force, a modern industrial nation.

Endangered species

The snow leopard and the giant panda are both endangered species, hunted almost to extinction.

1. YAK
2. SNOW LEOPARD
3. GIANT PANDA

A rural worker in China

Chinese farm workers often use this method for carrying produce. A strong wooden bar, called a yoke, rests across the back of the neck with a basket slung at each end.

0 500 Km
0 300 Miles

Amur
Xiao Hinggan Ling
Selenge
Kerulen
Qiqihar
Songhua
L. Khanka
Ulan Bator
Harbin
M a n c h u r i a
Da Hinggan Ling
Changchun
Jilin
Chongjin
Liao
Fushun
Shenyang
NORTH KOREA
Anshan
Pyongyang
A l t a i M t s.
MONGOLIA
G o b i
zungaria
Ürümqi
han
-505
Turfan Depression
Baotou
Hohhot
Beijing
Dalian
Seoul
Bosten Hu
Datong
Tianjin
SOUTH KOREA
Lop Nor
Shijiazhuang
Pusan
Tarim Basin
Huang
Taiyuan
Zibo
YELLOW SEA
Altun Shan
Qilian Shan
Yinchuan
Jinan
Qingdao
Xining
Huang
Xuzhou
Cheju
un S h a n
Qinghai Hu
Lanzhou
Zhengzhou
Tibetan Plateau
C H I N A
Xi'an
Luoyang
Huainan
Nanjing
Suzhou
Shanghai
EAST CHINA SEA
T i b e t
Lancang (Mekong)
Yalong
Han
Wuhan
Chang (Yangtze)
Hangzhou
Nu (Salween)
Jinsha
Lhasa
Yarlung Zangbo
Chengdu
Dongting Hu
Pcyang Hu
Wenzhou
Mt. Everest
29,028
Chang
Chongqing
Nanchang
Yibin
Xiangtan
Changsha
Fuzhou
Taipei
Guiyang
Hengyang
TAIWAN
Kunming
Liuzhou
Gaoxiong
Xi
Guangzhou
Nanning
HONG KONG (U.K.)
MACAO (Port.)
Zhanjiang
Hainan

In the east of China there are fertile plains, crossed by two great rivers. The Huang (Yellow River) flows into the Gulf of Bohai. The Chang, also known as the Yangtze, flows into the East China Sea. It is the world's third longest river, nearly 4000 miles in length. The valleys of these rivers have been farmed for thousands of years, and it was here that many great civilizations grew up in ancient times.

Most of China's cities lie in the eastern half of the country. These include the port of Shanghai, with a population of over seven million, and Beijing (Peking), the capital, with nearly six million. The northeast region, once known as Manchuria, is a center of mining and heavy industry.

The north of China is home to the Mongols and is a land of desert and rolling grasslands. The mountains and deserts of the northeast are inhabited by various tribal peoples. In the southeast, the vast Tibetan Plateau is bordered by the Himalayan range which includes some of the world's highest peaks.

Working in a silk factory
Silk is reeled and woven at this factory in Hangzhou, capital of Zhejiang province. China was already producing fine silks 3500 years ago. For centuries the art of silkworm breeding was kept secret from the rest of the world.

Xinjiang province, northwestern China
These Muslim men live in the northwestern region of Xinjiang. Most Chinese belong to the Han people, but there are in fact 56 ethnic groups in the country. These include Uighurs, Kazakhs, Uzbeks, and Mongols. Tibet is part of China, but many Tibetans want to be independent from China.

The Great Wall of China
The Great Wall (top) was built about 2200 years ago, to protect the ancient Chinese empire from northern warriors.

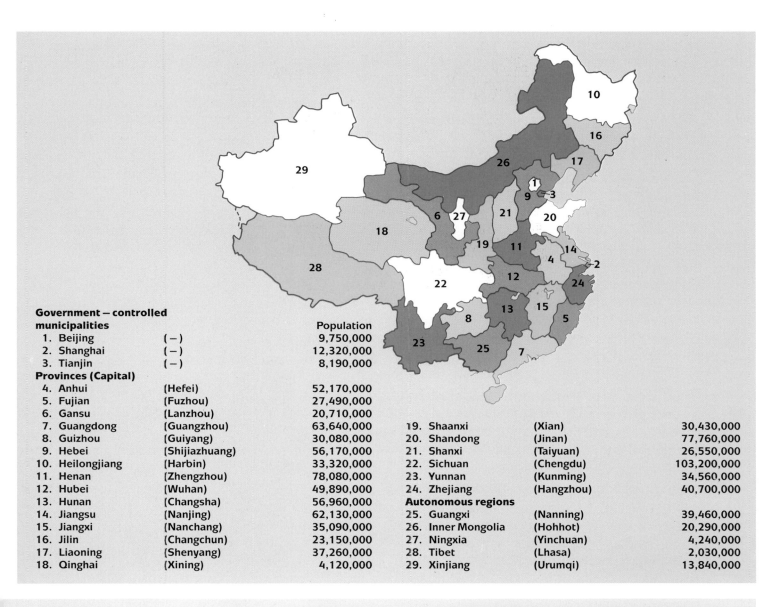

Government — controlled municipalities

		Population
1. Beijing	(−)	9,750,000
2. Shanghai	(−)	12,320,000
3. Tianjin	(−)	8,190,000

Provinces (Capital)

4. Anhui	(Hefei)	52,170,000
5. Fujian	(Fuzhou)	27,490,000
6. Gansu	(Lanzhou)	20,710,000
7. Guangdong	(Guangzhou)	63,640,000
8. Guizhou	(Guiyang)	30,080,000
9. Hebei	(Shijiazhuang)	56,170,000
10. Heilongjiang	(Harbin)	33,320,000
11. Henan	(Zhengzhou)	78,080,000
12. Hubei	(Wuhan)	49,890,000
13. Hunan	(Changsha)	56,960,000
14. Jiangsu	(Nanjing)	62,130,000
15. Jiangxi	(Nanchang)	35,090,000
16. Jilin	(Changchun)	23,150,000
17. Liaoning	(Shenyang)	37,260,000
18. Qinghai	(Xining)	4,120,000
19. Shaanxi	(Xian)	30,430,000
20. Shandong	(Jinan)	77,760,000
21. Shanxi	(Taiyuan)	26,550,000
22. Sichuan	(Chengdu)	103,200,000
23. Yunnan	(Kunming)	34,560,000
24. Zhejiang	(Hangzhou)	40,700,000

Autonomous regions

25. Guangxi	(Nanning)	39,460,000
26. Inner Mongolia	(Hohhot)	20,290,000
27. Ningxia	(Yinchuan)	4,240,000
28. Tibet	(Lhasa)	2,030,000
29. Xinjiang	(Urumqi)	13,840,000

The "Forbidden City"

Beijing (Peking) is the capital city of China. At its center is the old Imperial Palace, much of which was laid out in the fifteenth century. Its splendid temples and courtyards are known as the "Forbidden City." In the days of the emperors, ordinary Chinese citizens were not even allowed to approach its walls. Rule by the emperors came to an end in 1911, when China became a republic.

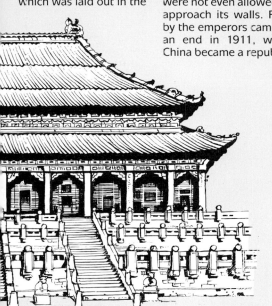

The Star Ferry, Hong Kong

Hong Kong is a British colony, which will return to Chinese control in 1997. Hong Kong and neighboring Macao are the most crowded places on Earth. Hong Kong is an important port and one of Asia's leading financial centers. The gleaming skyscrapers of its business district, Central, rise from an island harbor. It is linked by ferry *(above)* and tunnel with Kowloon, on the mainland. This region is a commercial center, with dense, high-rise housing.

JAPAN

Japan forms an archipelago in the Pacific comprising four main islands, Honshu, Hokkaido, Shikoku, and Kyushu, and over 3000 smaller, mostly uninhabited ones. This region is an earthquake zone and has over 50 active volcanoes. About 70 percent of the country is mountainous and covered with forests, and most people live on the coastal plains.

The climate is subtropical in the south and colder in the north. On Hokkaido there is snow for up to four months in the winter. The warm-water Kuroshio Current brings a rainy season to the south in June and early July.

Japan is one of the world's most successful industrial nations, producing cars, motorcycles, electrical goods, and over one third of the world's ships. All the raw materials to make these — such as iron ore, oil, and coal — have to be imported as Japan has almost no natural resources. Japan is also one of the major fishing nations, catching large amounts of tuna, squid, and octopus for its home market.

A Japanese garden
The Japanese are famous for their garden design. In the past many European gardens were modeled on Japanese styles with pagodas, bridges, teahouses, and stone lanterns arranged around a pool or stream. Over the centuries growing trees has also developed into a sophisticated art in Japan — especially miniature trees like the bonsai, which are grown in pots.

Sumo wrestling
Sumo wrestling is the top spectator sport in Japan. Here, two Sumo wrestlers face each other in the ring, ready to start the contest. Each has to try to force his opponent out of the ring, which is marked by a circular rope on the ground. The wrestlers are very strong, weighing over 330 pounds each.

Originally, Sumo wrestling matches were held in Shinto shrines (Shinto is the old religion of Japan). The referee still dresses like a Shinto priest.

The Japanese at work

In large Japanese corporations today it is quite common for workers to participate in morning exercise routines on the factory floor. Many Japanese employees also wear a company uniform and take pride in their teamwork.

The people of Japan have become known worldwide as hardworking and efficient, and are world leaders in the electronics field. Robots and advanced computers are used to produce the latest in household technology, such as microwave ovens, camcorders, video cassette recorders, and stereos.

The tea ceremony

A mother and daughter conducting a tea ceremony. Although Japan is a modern westernized society, old traditions are carefully preserved. The tea ceremony is an ancient ritual that many Japanese women still continue to learn and practice. The bitter, green tea is served in delicate china and drunk slowly and reverently.

Harvesting rice

Farmers in this rice field are gathering the rice into bundles to dry before threshing. Farming equipment is specially designed for Japanese farms, which are very small. Only 15 percent of the land in Japan is suitable for cultivation.

La Perouse Strait

C. Soya
Rebun
Rishiri
Wakkanai

0   300 Km
0   200 Miles

Asahikawa

Ishikari

Hokkaido

Sapporo

Kushiro

Okushiri

Hakodate

C. Erimo

Tsugaru Str.

C. Shiriya

Aomori

Akita

SEA OF

JAPAN

Sendai

Sado

JAPAN

Niigata

C. Suzu

Koriyama

Iwaki

Shinano

Nagano

Utsunomiya

Kanazawa

Toyama

Maebashi

Tone

Honshu

Tokyo

Gifu

Kawasaki
Yokohama

Chiba

Oki Is.

Mt. Fuji▲
12,388

Yokosuka

L. Biwa

Kyoto

Nagoya

Shizuoka

Tsu
Shima

Himeji

Okayama

Toyohashi

Hamamatsu

Hiroshima

Kobe

Shimonoseki

Kure

Takamatsu

Osaka

Sakai
Wakayama

Kitakyushu

Matsuyama

Tokushima

Fukuoka

Kochi

Sasebo

Oita

C. Shio

Nagasaki

Kumamoto

Shikoku

Kyushu

Kagoshima

Osumi Is.   *Tanega*

Yaku

Amami

Tokuno   *Ryūkyū*

Islands

Okinawa

AFRICA

Africa is the second largest continent, stretching south from the Mediterranean Sea and lying between the Atlantic and the Indian Oceans. It is a land of infinite contrast. Much of northern Africa is covered by the Sahara, the biggest and hottest desert in the world, larger in size than the whole of Australia. In western and central regions, large areas of the coast are covered by dense tropical rainforests.

The Great Rift Valley runs from the Red Sea south to Malawi. East of the Rift are the mountain ranges of Ethiopia, Kenya, and Tanzania, including the highest mountain peak in Africa, Kilimanjaro at 19,340 feet. High plateaus in eastern and southern Africa are covered by rolling grasslands, known as savanna, home to much of Africa's abundant wildlife.

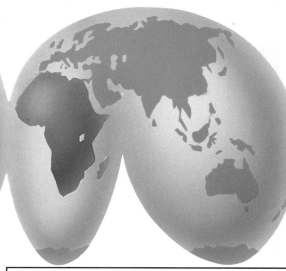

Open grassland, or *veldt*, in Drakensberg, on the border between South Africa and Lesotho.

Africa
Highest point Kilimanjaro (Tanzania) 19,340ft. (5895m.) above sea level
Lowest point Lake Assal (Djibouti) 509ft. (155m.) below sea level

Longest river Nile (Egypt) 4145mi. (6671km.)
Largest lake Victoria (Kenya/Uganda/Tanzania) 26,828 sq.mi. (69,484 sq.km.)

MOROCCO
Area 177,070 sq. miles (458,775 sq. km.)
Population 25,500,000
Capital Rabat
Chief products Clay, lead, marble, cement, food, soap, leather, textiles, almonds

GHANA
Area 92,100 sq. miles (238,537 sq. km.)
Population 15,000,000
Capital Accra
Chief products Textiles, bauxite, diamonds, gold, manganese, cacao, coffee

LIBYA
Area 685,524 sq. miles (1,775,500 sq. km.)
Population 4,200,000
Capital Tripoli
Chief products Oil, citrus fruits, dates, barley, olives, livestock, wheat

ALGERIA
Area 919,595 sq. miles (2,381,741 sq. km.)
Population 25,600,000
Capital Algiers
Chief products Iron ore, oil, phosphates, fruit, grain, vegetables, wine

NIGERIA
Area 356,669 sq. miles (923,768 sq. km.)
Population 118,800,000
Capital Lagos
Chief products Oil, tin, limestone, rubber, rice, chemicals, beans, cacao

EGYPT
Area 385,229 sq. miles (997,738 sq. km.)
Population 54,700,000
Capital Cairo
Chief products Iron ore, oil, manganese, salt, fish, cement, fertilizers, steel

ETHIOPIA
Area 483,123 sq. miles (1,251,282 sq. km.)
Population 51,700,000
Capital Addis Ababa
Chief products Barley, beans, coffee, cotton, hides and skins, livestock, lumber

ZAIRE
Area 905,365 sq. miles (2,344,885 sq. km.)
Population 36,600,000
Capital Kinshasa
Chief products Cement, industrial diamonds, oil, coffee, cotton, copper, gold

IVORY COAST
Area 124,503 sq. miles (322,462 sq. km.)
Population 12,600,000
Capital Abidjan
Chief products Textiles, fruit, electrical equipment, ships, textiles, lumber

CAMEROON
Area 183,569 sq. miles (475,442 sq. km.)
Population 11,100,000
Capital Yaoundé
Chief products Aluminum, oil, lumber, natural rubber, bananas, cassava, cacao

SUDAN
Area 967,500 sq. miles (2,505,813 sq. km.)
Population 25,200,000
Capital Khartoum
Chief products Cotton, corn, dates, hides, skins, melons, peanuts, salt

KENYA
Area 224,081 sq. miles (580,367 sq. km.)
Population 24,600,000
Capital Nairobi
Chief products Coffee, corn, tea, sisal, sugarcane, cement, chemicals

UGANDA
Area 91,343 sq. miles (231,860 sq. km.)
Population 18,000,000
Capital Kampala
Chief products Copper, bananas, coffee, cotton, sweet potatoes, tea

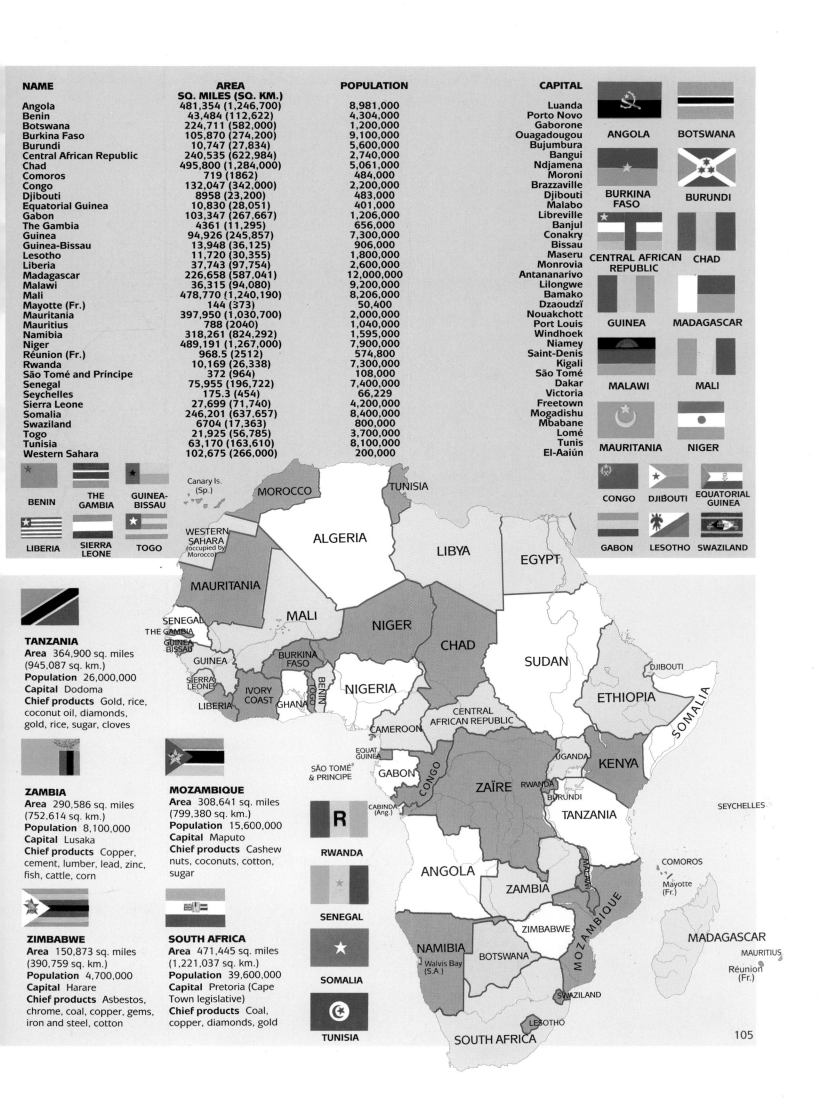

NAME	AREA SQ. MILES (SQ. KM.)	POPULATION	CAPITAL
Angola	481,354 (1,246,700)	8,981,000	Luanda
Benin	43,484 (112,622)	4,304,000	Porto Novo
Botswana	224,711 (582,000)	1,200,000	Gaborone
Burkina Faso	105,870 (274,200)	9,100,000	Ouagadougou
Burundi	10,747 (27,834)	5,600,000	Bujumbura
Central African Republic	240,535 (622,984)	2,740,000	Bangui
Chad	495,800 (1,284,000)	5,061,000	Ndjamena
Comoros	719 (1862)	484,000	Moroni
Congo	132,047 (342,000)	2,200,000	Brazzaville
Djibouti	8958 (23,200)	483,000	Djibouti
Equatorial Guinea	10,830 (28,051)	401,000	Malabo
Gabon	103,347 (267,667)	1,206,000	Libreville
The Gambia	4361 (11,295)	656,000	Banjul
Guinea	94,926 (245,857)	7,300,000	Conakry
Guinea-Bissau	13,948 (36,125)	906,000	Bissau
Lesotho	11,720 (30,355)	1,800,000	Maseru
Liberia	37,743 (97,754)	2,600,000	Monrovia
Madagascar	226,658 (587,041)	12,000,000	Antananarivo
Malawi	36,315 (94,080)	9,200,000	Lilongwe
Mali	478,770 (1,240,190)	8,206,000	Bamako
Mayotte (Fr.)	144 (373)	50,400	Dzaoudzï
Mauritania	397,950 (1,030,700)	2,000,000	Nouakchott
Mauritius	788 (2040)	1,040,000	Port Louis
Namibia	318,261 (824,292)	1,595,000	Windhoek
Niger	489,191 (1,267,000)	7,900,000	Niamey
Réunion (Fr.)	968.5 (2512)	574,800	Saint-Denis
Rwanda	10,169 (26,338)	7,300,000	Kigali
São Tomé and Príncipe	372 (964)	108,000	São Tomé
Senegal	75,955 (196,722)	7,400,000	Dakar
Seychelles	175.3 (454)	66,229	Victoria
Sierra Leone	27,699 (71,740)	4,200,000	Freetown
Somalia	246,201 (637,657)	8,400,000	Mogadishu
Swaziland	6704 (17,363)	800,000	Mbabane
Togo	21,925 (56,785)	3,700,000	Lomé
Tunisia	63,170 (163,610)	8,100,000	Tunis
Western Sahara	102,675 (266,000)	200,000	El-Aaiún

ANGOLA **BOTSWANA** **BURKINA FASO** **BURUNDI** **CENTRAL AFRICAN REPUBLIC** **CHAD** **GUINEA** **MADAGASCAR** **MALAWI** **MALI** **MAURITANIA** **NIGER**

BENIN **THE GAMBIA** **GUINEA-BISSAU** **LIBERIA** **SIERRA LEONE** **TOGO**

CONGO **DJIBOUTI** **EQUATORIAL GUINEA** **GABON** **LESOTHO** **SWAZILAND**

TANZANIA
Area 364,900 sq. miles (945,087 sq. km.)
Population 26,000,000
Capital Dodoma
Chief products Gold, rice, coconut oil, diamonds, gold, rice, sugar, cloves

ZAMBIA
Area 290,586 sq. miles (752,614 sq. km.)
Population 8,100,000
Capital Lusaka
Chief products Copper, cement, lumber, lead, zinc, fish, cattle, corn

ZIMBABWE
Area 150,873 sq. miles (390,759 sq. km.)
Population 4,700,000
Capital Harare
Chief products Asbestos, chrome, coal, copper, gems, iron and steel, cotton

MOZAMBIQUE
Area 308,641 sq. miles (799,380 sq. km.)
Population 15,600,000
Capital Maputo
Chief products Cashew nuts, coconuts, cotton, sugar

SOUTH AFRICA
Area 471,445 sq. miles (1,221,037 sq. km.)
Population 39,600,000
Capital Pretoria (Cape Town legislative)
Chief products Coal, copper, diamonds, gold

RWANDA **SENEGAL** **SOMALIA** **TUNISIA**

105

NORTHERN AFRICA

North Africa is dominated by the Sahara, which stretches 3000 miles from the Atlantic coast in Mauritania across to the Red Sea in Sudan. It is the largest desert in the world; moreover, drought and destructive farming methods are causing it to expand southwards at the rate of about six miles a year. The climate along the Mediterranean coast enables crops such as dates and fruit to be grown, particularly in the foothills of the Atlas Mountains in the northwest. Huge irrigation systems are being developed by oil-rich Libya to pump water from deep beneath the desert to the fertile coastal areas 560 miles distant. However, farther south in Sudan and the highlands of Ethiopia, crop failures and drought have caused widespread famine.

Traditionally the Arab world has had a great influence on northern Africa, particularly in Egypt. The people of the region are mostly Muslim, and Arabic is widely spoken.

The River Nile
Much of Egypt is desert land which cannot support vegetation. The fertile regions on either side of the River Nile and in the Nile delta (*seen here*) form the major agricultural areas.

The River Nile is controlled by the Aswan Dam, completed in 1965, and now flows steadily all year, providing a constant supply of water for irrigation. Before the dam was built, the Nile regularly flooded its banks, washing nutrient-rich mud onto the land.

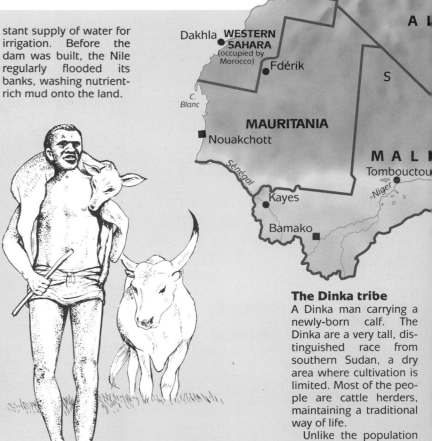

Madeira
(Port.)

Ceuta (Sp.) Meli
Tangier● (Sp
Rabat● Fès
Casablanca●
Marrakesh● **MOROCCO**

Canary Islands
(Sp.)

El Aaiún●

Dakhla● **WESTERN SAHARA**
(occupied by Morocco)
Fdérik●

A

S

C. Blanc

MAURITANIA
Nouakchott■

M A L I
Tombouctou●
Sénégal
Niger
Kayes●
Bamako■

The Dinka tribe
A Dinka man carrying a newly-born calf. The Dinka are a very tall, distinguished race from southern Sudan, a dry area where cultivation is limited. Most of the people are cattle herders, maintaining a traditional way of life.

Unlike the population

Ethiopia's famine

Ethiopia has been hit by severe drought for many years in succession. Lack of rain has meant that crops and livestock have perished, leaving many millions of people starving. There was a severe drought in 1973, but it was little publicized. In 1974 a Communist revolution overthrew Haile Selassie, who was the emperor at that time, and since then drought and warfare have together caused widespread suffering. The wars being fought by the two provinces of Tigre and Eritrea in northern Ethiopia, in an attempt to win independence from Addis Ababa's rule, have destroyed agriculture and made transport of food and medical supplies nearly impossible.

The devastating famine of 1985 was brought to the attention of the whole world, particularly by the pop music charity Band Aid, which organized an international music festival called Live Aid. The revenue from this en-

A Moroccan *souk*

All major towns in Morocco feature a bazaar, or *souk*, selling local and imported goods in noisy, colorful, and pungent surroundings. Exotic items are sold including brassware, jewelry, spices, and perfumes, and fresh local produce is available too. Other activities include leather tanning and wool dying.

abled international relief agencies such as the Red Cross and Oxfam to provide medical supplies, food, and shelter to many of the most affected areas.

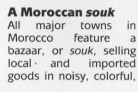

of the north, the people of southern Sudan, such as the Dinka and the Nuer, are not Muslim and do not speak Arabic. Conflict arising from these differences led to civil war in the 1980's. The spread of Islam and Arabic from the north continues to be a threat to the people of the south.

giers
Annaba
Tunis
ran Constantine
Sousse
tains
Sfax
Chott Djerid
TUNISIA
Tripoli
Misratah
Benghazi
Alexandria
Port Said
Qattara
Depression ▼-436
Cairo
Suez
Sinai
ERIA
L i b y a n
Ghudamis
LIBYA
Asyut
EGYPT
Marzuq
D e s e r t
Aswan
A
H
Ahaggar
▲Tahat
9574
R
L. Nasser
Tamanrasset
Tibesti
▲Emi Koussi
11,204
Nubian
Desert
Port
Sudan
RED
Aïr.
Atbara
Atbara
Asmera
NIGER
CHAD
Omdurman
Kassala
Eritrea
SEA
Agades
Khartoum
Blue Nile
Gonder
Danakil
DJIBOUTI
Ras
Asir
Niamey
Zinder
L. Chad
Abéché
Darfur
El Obeid
White Nile
L. Tana
Djibouti
Berbera
Ndjamena
SUDAN
**Addis
Ababa**
Dire
Dawa
Hargeisa
Chari
S u d d
Jima
ETHIOPIA
Ogaden
Sarh
Shebele
SOMALIA
Juba
Juba

0   1200 Km
0   800 Miles

WESTERN, CENTRAL, AND EASTERN AFRICA

In western Africa, the Gulf of Guinea is bordered by many relatively small countries. Agriculture is important, and crops such as cocoa, palm oil, and peanuts, as well as hardwood trees are grown for export. Nigeria, the most populous country in Africa, has benefitted from the discovery of large oil reserves in the late 1950's. Oil revenues have been used to finance new industries such as petrochemical production, steelmaking, and vehicle manufacture.

Dense tropical rainforests lie across central Africa, through which flows the River Zaïre. Like much of Africa, the countries of this region are made up of peoples of many different tribes — in Zaïre, for example, over 250 different local languages are spoken. To the east of the Great Rift Valley the flat grasslands of Tanzania and Kenya are sparsely populated by the Masai and other cattle herders. The climate in this region is particularly suited to growing coffee and tea, which are major exports.

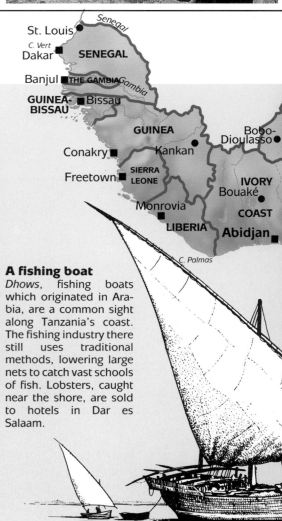

Lagos, Nigeria

Nigeria has a population of over 118 million, the largest in Africa, made up of 250 different groups and tribes including the Hausa, Yoruba, and Ibo peoples. Lagos, the capital, is a thriving port on the southwest coast. The heart of the city, Lagos island, contains the administrative sector and is linked to the mainland and other islands by road bridges.

Huge oil reserves, discovered in the 1950's, have enabled Nigeria to build roads and ports and set up new industries. Despite this industrial development, Nigeria is still unable to produce enough food for its rapidly increasing population.

A fishing boat

Dhows, fishing boats which originated in Arabia, are a common sight along Tanzania's coast. The fishing industry there still uses traditional methods, lowering large nets to catch vast schools of fish. Lobsters, caught near the shore, are sold to hotels in Dar es Salaam.

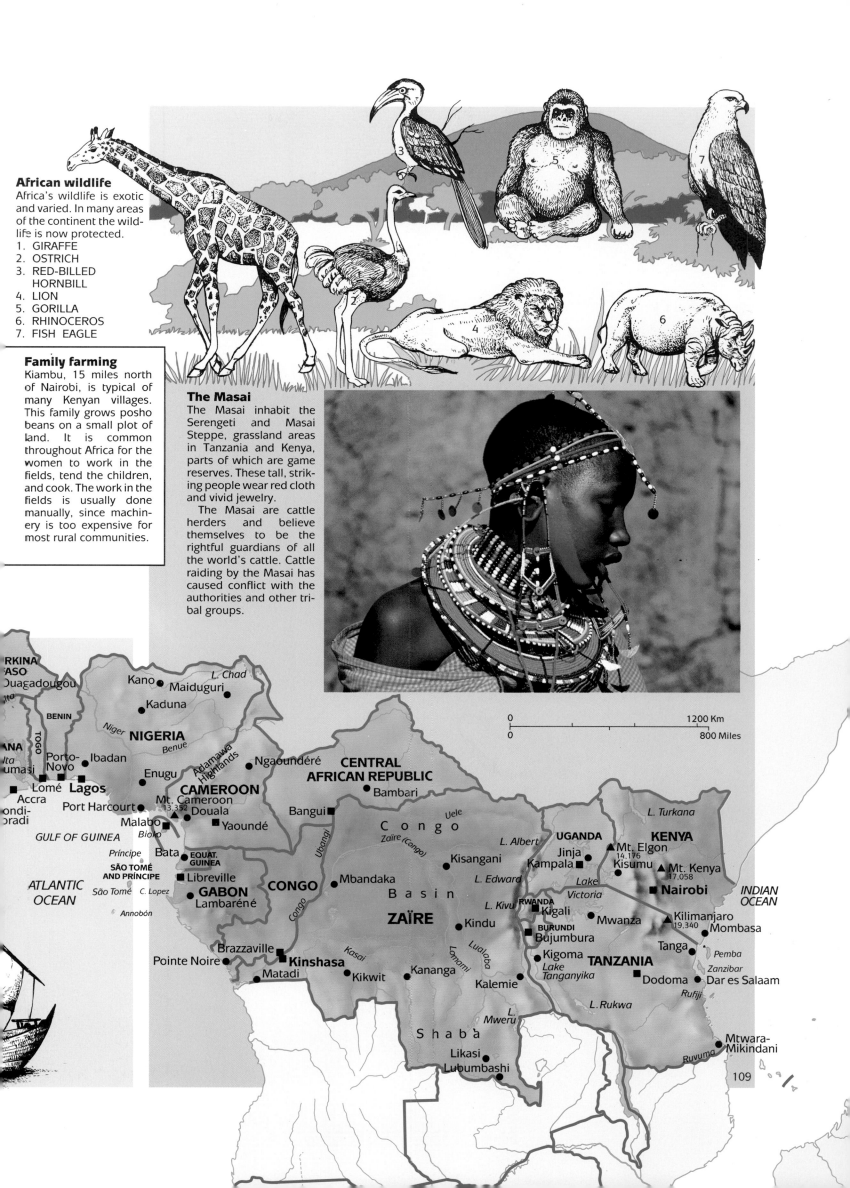

African wildlife

Africa's wildlife is exotic and varied. In many areas of the continent the wildlife is now protected.

1. GIRAFFE
2. OSTRICH
3. RED-BILLED HORNBILL
4. LION
5. GORILLA
6. RHINOCEROS
7. FISH EAGLE

Family farming

Kiambu, 15 miles north of Nairobi, is typical of many Kenyan villages. This family grows posho beans on a small plot of land. It is common throughout Africa for the women to work in the fields, tend the children, and cook. The work in the fields is usually done manually, since machinery is too expensive for most rural communities.

The Masai

The Masai inhabit the Serengeti and Masai Steppe, grassland areas in Tanzania and Kenya, parts of which are game reserves. These tall, striking people wear red cloth and vivid jewelry.

The Masai are cattle herders and believe themselves to be the rightful guardians of all the world's cattle. Cattle raiding by the Masai has caused conflict with the authorities and other tribal groups.

0   1200 Km
0   800 Miles

RKINA
ASO
Ouagadougou
Ita

Kano
Maiduguri
Kaduna
L. Chad

BENIN
TOGO
Niger
NIGERIA
Benue

ANA
Ita
umasi
Porto-
Novo
Ibadan
Enugu
Adamawa Highlands
Ngaoundéré

**CENTRAL
AFRICAN REPUBLIC**
Bambari

Lomé **Lagos**
Accra
Ondi-
oradi
Port Harcourt
Mt. Cameroon
13,352
Douala
CAMEROON
Bangui
C o n g o
Uele

Malabo
Yaoundé
Ubangi
Zaïre (Congo)

GULF OF GUINEA
Bioko
Kisangani

L. Albert
UGANDA
Jinja
Kampala
KENYA
L. Turkana
Mt. Elgon
14,176
Kisumu
Mt. Kenya
17,058

Príncipe
Bata
**EQUAT.
GUINEA**
Mbandaka
B a s i n
L. Edward
Lake
Victoria

**SÃO TOMÉ
AND PRÍNCIPE**
Libreville
GABON
Lambaréné
São Tomé C. Lopez
CONGO

_ATLANTIC
OCEAN_
Annobón

ZAÏRE
Kindu
L. Kivu
RWANDA
Kigali

Mwanza
Kilimanjaro
19,340

Nairobi
_INDIAN
OCEAN_
Mombasa

Brazzaville
Kasai
BURUNDI
Bujumbura
Tanga
Pemba

Pointe Noire
Kinshasa
Matadi
Kikwit
Kananga
Lomami
Lualaba
Kigoma
Lake
Tanganyika
TANZANIA
Dodoma
Dar es Salaam
Zanzibar

Congo
Kalemie
Rufiji

L.
Mweru
L. Rukwa

S h a b a

Likasi
Lubumbashi

Mtwara-
Mikindani
Ruvuma

109

SOUTHERN AFRICA

Angola, Zambia, Mozambique, and the countries farther south are all part of southern Africa. The landscape across this region varies from the hot, dry areas of the Namib Desert in Namibia and the Kalahari in Botswana, to the vast, open grasslands of the *veldt* in South Africa and the lush low-lying plains which cover most of Mozambique.

The economies of most of the southern African countries rely heavily on the wealth resulting from the export of minerals. This region contains one of the greatest concentrations of valuable mineral resources in the world. Botswana, South Africa, and Zimbabwe have some of the world's richest diamond deposits as well as huge coal reserves.

South Africa is the richest and most developed of all the countries in this region, but it is politically unstable because of a system called "apartheid," which keeps its black majority population separate and unequal from the white minority. Conditions are improving, but many countries still refuse to trade with South Africa because of apartheid.

Kokerboom Forest, Namibia
The Kokerboom tree is also known as the "quiver tree," because the Bushmen used to make pincushion-type quivers for their arrows from its fibrous core. The trees thrive in the arid land of central Namibia because they store water and can resist drought for years.

Agriculture in Zambia
In order to provide food for Africa's ever-growing population, agriculture must be developed. One option is to improve farming techniques in the villages. Alternatively, large-scale projects can be adopted, such as the Mpongwe scheme in Zambia which produces soybeans.

Bushmen of the Kalahari
Bushmen women from the Kalahari region making jewelry from tiny fragments of ostrich shells.

Mineral resources in southern Africa

Rich mineral deposits exist throughout southern and southwestern Africa. This diamond mine in Angola is one of many in this region.

Zimbabwe and South Africa both mine gold. However the industry is much larger in South Africa where Johannesburg is the world's gold mining center.

Mining for other elements is widespread, particularly in South Africa where platinum, uranium, and coal are produced. However, the recycling of metals such as aluminum and steel is now becoming common throughout the world. This saves energy and resources but is reducing the demand for some minerals and so also diminishing their value.

The wildlife of southern Africa

A huge variety of wildlife is found in southern Africa. In the grasslands of South Africa the many species of antelope, such as the eland and oryx, are hunted by lions and cheetahs. Huge herds of wildebeest roam the plains, and groups of giraffes and elephants wander around the waterholes. Leopards live in mountainous regions including those in Malawi and Zimbabwe. In the Okavango Swamp in Botswana, hippopotamuses and crocodiles are abundant.

Madagascar is separated from mainland Africa by a considerable distance which has caused the animals there to evolve independently. A great number of species are unique to the island, including many varieties of the monkey-like lemur.

1. HYENA
2. CHIMPANZEE
3. AARDVARK
4. LEMUR

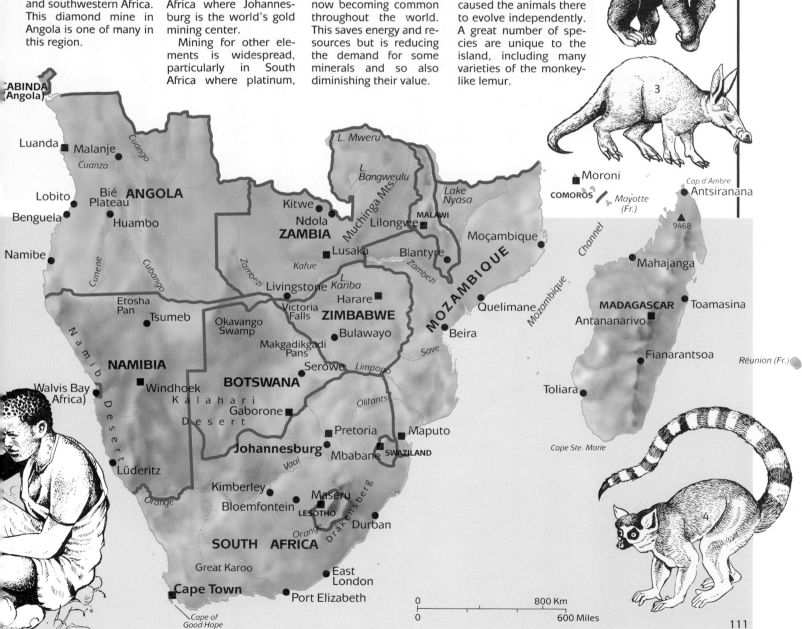

OCEANIA

Oceania is the name given to the region which includes Australia, New Zealand and the islands which are scattered across the Pacific Ocean. These islands are grouped into three areas: Melanesia, Micronesia, and Polynesia. No one knows exactly how many Pacific islands there are, but it is estimated that the total lies between twenty and thirty thousand. Some are coral islands while others, such as Hawaii, are volcanoes rising above the sea.

One of Australia's most famous attractions lies not on the land but in the sea. It is the beautiful Great Barrier Reef, which stretches for 1250 miles off the northeast coast. Farther south New Zealand's two main islands have a cooler, wetter climate than Australia, and a landscape which varies from rugged mountains to rolling, green plains.

Oceania
Highest point Mount Cook (New Zealand) 12,349ft. (3764m.) above sea level
Lowest point Lake Eyre (Australia) 52ft. (16m.) below sea level
Longest river Murray-Darling (Australia) 2330mi. (3750km.)
Largest lake Lake Eyre (Australia) 3700 sq.mi. (9500 sq.km.)

AUSTRALIA
Area 2,966,151 sq. miles (7,682,300 sq. km.)
Population 17,100,000
Capital Canberra (pop. 257,850)
Currency Australian Dollar
Official language(s) English
Chief products Sheep, beef cattle, cereal, fruit, wine, wool, minerals, salt, coal, bauxite, wheat
Exports Wool, lamb, beef, cereals, dairy products, machinery, minerals, tobacco
Imports Alcoholic drinks, coal, oil, food, machinery
AUSTRALIAN STATES AND TERRITORIES
New South Wales
Area 309,500 sq. miles (801,600 sq. km.)
Population 5,612,244
Capital Sydney (pop. 3,472,700)
Victoria
Area 87,800 sq. miles (227,600 sq. km.)
Population 4,208,946

Capital Melbourne (pop. 2,931,900)
Queensland
Area 666,875 sq. miles (1,727,200 sq. km.)
Population 2,676,765
Capital Brisbane (pop. 1,196,000)
South Australia
Area 380,000 sq. miles (984,000 sq. km.)
Population 1,394,154
Capital Adelaide (pop. 1,003,800)
Western Australia
Area 975,000 sq. miles (2,525,500 sq. km.)
Population 1,500,507
Capital Perth (pop. 1,050,400)
Tasmania
Area 26,180 sq. miles (67,800 sq. km.)
Population 447,941
Capital Hobart (pop. 179,000)
Northern Territory
Area 520,000 sq. miles (1,346,200 sq. km.)
Population 156,674
Capital Darwin (pop. 74,800)
Australian Capital Territory
Area 927 sq. miles (2400 sq. km.)
Population 266,088
Capital Canberra

NEW ZEALAND
Area 103,415 sq. miles (267,844 sq. km.)
Population 3,349,200
Capital Wellington (pop. 324,400)
Largest cities Auckland (829,200)
Christchurch (299,400)
Dunedin (106,600)
Hamilton (102,600)
Currency New Zealand Dollar
Official language(s) English, Maori
Chief products Sheep, wool, lamb, beef and dairy cattle, hardwood timber, minerals (especially coal, iron, sand), wheat, poultry, natural gas
Exports Iron ore, wheat, wool, live sheep and lambs, oil, oil products, beef, butter, kiwi fruit
Imports Machinery, electrical equipment, vehicles, iron and steel, textiles

PAPUA NEW GUINEA
Area 178,655 sq. miles (462,840 sq. km.)
Population 3,479,400
Capital Port Moresby
Official language(s) English (Pidgin English and Hiri Motu are also spoken)
Chief products Copper, silver, gold, minerals, oil and gas, paint, plywood, cocoa, copra, tea, coffee

FIJI
Official name Matanitu Ko Fiti
Area 7075 sq. miles (18,330 sq. km.)
Population 800,000
Capital Suva
Official language(s) English and Fijian
Chief products Sugarcane and molasses, coconuts, ginger, copra, fruit, fish, vegetables, rice, lumber

NAME	AREA SQ. MILES (SQ. KM.)	POPULATION	CAPITAL
Cook Islands (N.Z.)	113 (293)	17,185	Avarua
French Polynesia	1520 (3940)	188,814	Papeete
Guam (U.S.A.)	212 (549)	129,254	Agaña
Kiribati	284 (684)	66,000	Tarawa
Marshall Islands (U.S.A.)	70 (180)	34,923	Majuro
The Federated States of Micronesia (U.S.A.)	127 (330)	86,094	Kolonia
Nauru	8.2 (21.3)	8042	Yaren
New Caledonia (Fr.)	7358 (19,058)	153,000	Noumea
Niue (N.Z.)	100 (259)	2190	Alofi
Norfolk Is. (Aus.)	13.3 (34.5)	1977	Kingston
Northern Marianas (U.S.A.)	184 (476)	22,000	Saipan
Palau (U.S.A.)	142 (367)	14,106	Koror
Pitcairn Islands (U.K.)	17.25 (45)	57	—
Samoa (U.S.A.)	76 (196)	34,500	Pago Pago
Solomon Islands	11,500 (29,790)	285,796	Honiara
Tonga	270 (699)	111,000	Nuku'alofa
Tuvalu	9.5 (24.6)	8229	Funafuti
Vanuatu	5700 (14,763)	140,154	Port Vila
Wallis and Futuna Is. (Fr.)	106 (274)	13,100	Mata-Utu
Western Samoa	1095 (2840)	163,000	Apia

KIRIBATI   TONGA

NAURU   TUVALU

PALAU   VANUATU

SOLOMON IS.   WESTERN SAMOA

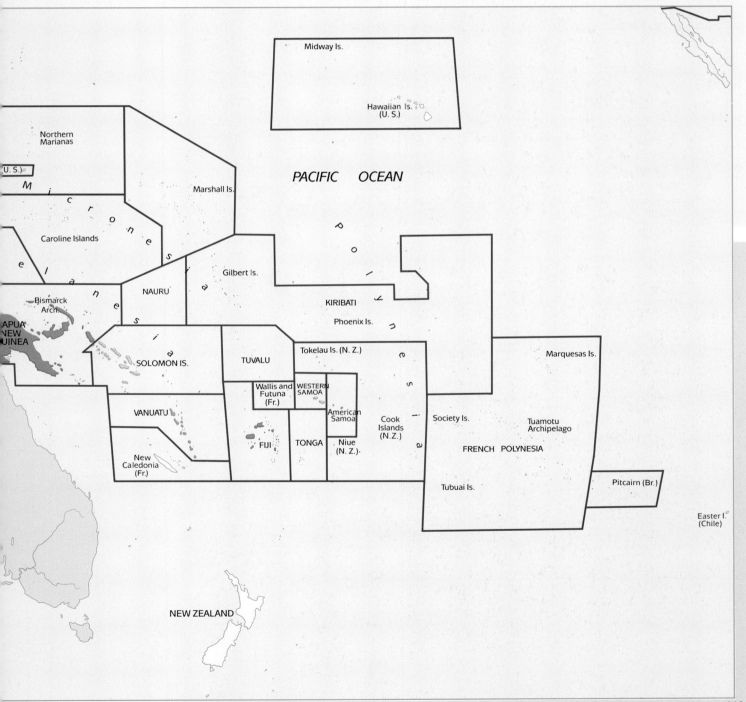

AUSTRALIA

Australia is made up of five mainland states, two territories, and the island state of Tasmania. The arid interior of the continent, known as the outback, is virtually uninhabited, but in areas where water can be found there are huge cattle ranches and sheep farms — Australia is the world's largest producer of wool.

Eighty percent of the Australian population lives in cities, almost all of which are located in the fertile area in the south-east between Adelaide and Brisbane, and around Perth in Western Australia. Fewer than 50,000 Aborigines, the native people of Australia, survive. Some cling to their traditional ways of life, but most have moved to the cities, or live on lands set aside for them by the government.

Australia is one of the world's largest mineral producers — bauxite (aluminum ore), copper, iron ore, and coal are all found in abundance in north and west Australia.

A sheep auction
Australia is the world's chief wool producing country. Here, Merino sheep are being sold at an auction. The Merino is specially bred for its fine quality wool.

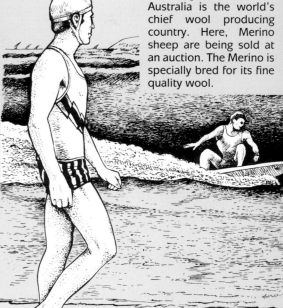

Ayers Rock
Ayers Rock is Australia's most famous landmark. It is nearly two miles long and five and a half miles round. It lies in the middle of the vast flat desert lands of central Australia. The Rock is sacred to the Aborigines — inside it are caves with paintings and carvings on the walls which depict stories of their ancestors. It is known to the Aborigines as Uluru.

Surfing off Bondi beach
A surf lifeguard on one of the golden beaches near Sydney in southeastern Australia. Beaches such as Bondi and Tamarama are only five miles from the city center.

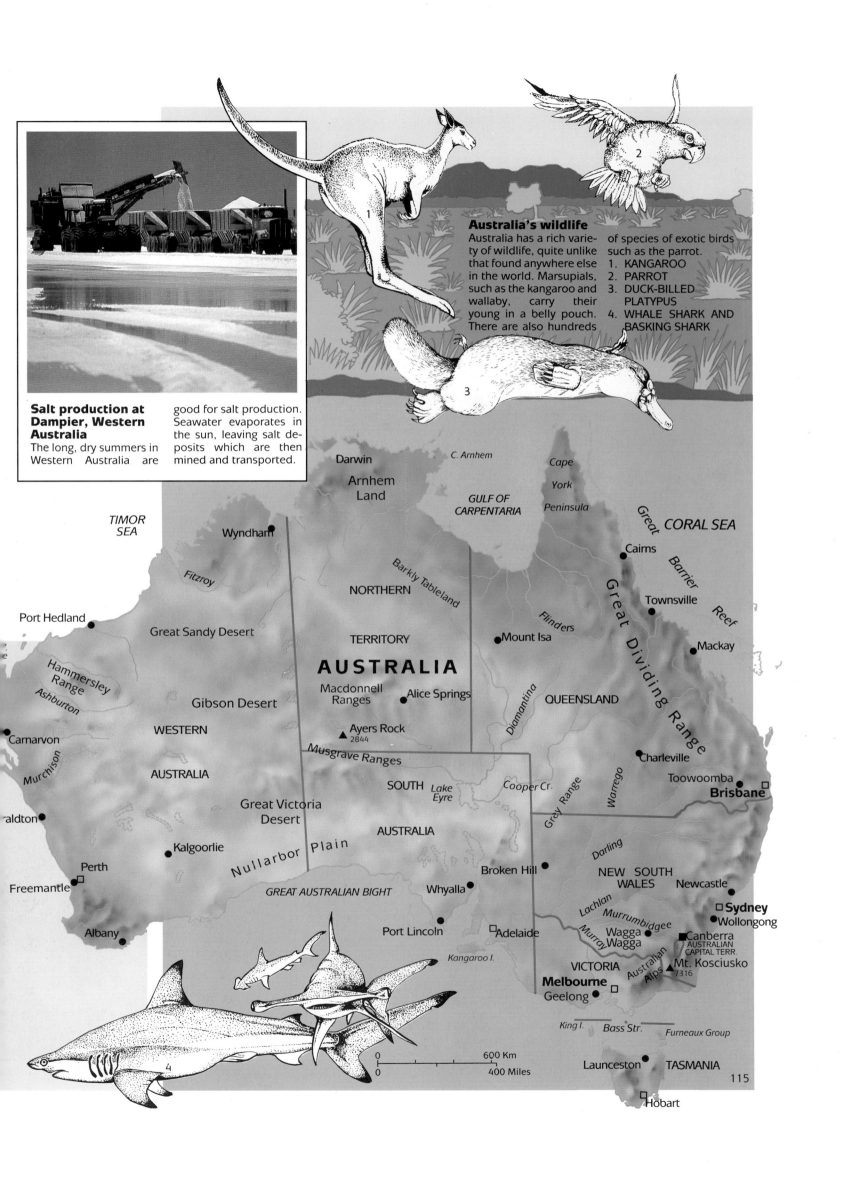

Salt production at Dampier, Western Australia

The long, dry summers in Western Australia are good for salt production. Seawater evaporates in the sun, leaving salt deposits which are then mined and transported.

Australia's wildlife

Australia has a rich variety of wildlife, quite unlike that found anywhere else in the world. Marsupials, such as the kangaroo and wallaby, carry their young in a belly pouch. There are also hundreds of species of exotic birds such as the parrot.
1. KANGAROO
2. PARROT
3. DUCK-BILLED PLATYPUS
4. WHALE SHARK AND BASKING SHARK

TIMOR SEA

Darwin

C. Arnhem

Cape York Peninsula

GULF OF CARPENTARIA

CORAL SEA

Arnhem Land

Wyndham

Fitzroy

Barkly Tableland

NORTHERN

Cairns

Great Barrier Reef

Port Hedland

Great Sandy Desert

TERRITORY

Townsville

Hammersley Range

Ashburton

Gibson Desert

AUSTRALIA

Macdonnell Ranges

Alice Springs

Flinders

Mount Isa

Mackay

Great Dividing Range

Carnarvon

WESTERN

Ayers Rock
2844

QUEENSLAND

Diamantina

Murchison

AUSTRALIA

Musgrave Ranges

SOUTH

Lake Eyre

Cooper Cr.

Charleville

...aldton

Great Victoria Desert

AUSTRALIA

Warrego

Gray Range

Toowoomba

Brisbane

Kalgoorlie

Nullarbor Plain

Broken Hill

Darling

NEW SOUTH WALES

Newcastle

Perth

Freemantle

GREAT AUSTRALIAN BIGHT

Whyalla

Lachlan

Murrumbidgee

Sydney

Wollongong

Albany

Port Lincoln

Adelaide

Wagga Wagga

Murray

Canberra
AUSTRALIAN CAPITAL TERR.

Kangaroo I.

VICTORIA

Australian Alps

Mt. Kosciusko
7316

Melbourne

Geelong

King I.

Bass Str.

Furneaux Group

0   600 Km

0   400 Miles

Launceston

TASMANIA

Hobart

NEW ZEALAND

New Zealand consists of two large islands and a number of smaller ones. Parts of North Island are volcanically active, with bubbling mud pools and geysers which shoot boiling water up to 300 feet in the air. As well as being a tourist attraction, the geysers produce steam which is used to generate electricity. The lower mountain slopes and green plains on South Island provide ideal grazing land for sheep.

Most of the population of New Zealand lives on North Island and is descended from the Europeans who settled it in the nineteenth and twentieth centuries. The native inhabitants of the country, the Maoris, are now in the minority.

New Zealand's economy is based on agriculture — especially the export of dairy produce, meat, and specialized foods such as the kiwi fruit. Recently, reserves of natural gas have been discovered off the west coast, and wood pulp and iron export industries have been established.

Wellington

This is the port at Wellington, the capital of New Zealand, which is situated at the southern tip of North Island. It is characterized by steep hills, earthquakes, and year-round gusting winds — its nickname is the "windy city." From the port, the Picton Ferry provides a link between North and South Islands. About 60 percent of all exports, primarily dairy produce and lamb, is shipped in huge refrigerated containers from here to Europe, the U.S.A., and Japan. The remainder is transported from Auckland farther north.

The Maoris

Wood carving is a traditional craft of the Maoris, the original inhabitants who came by canoe from other Pacific islands to New Zealand in about A.D. 800. The wood carvings, which show aspects of traditional Maori life, are mostly produced today for sale to tourists. Another traditional craft is the fashioning of jewelry, made from semiprecious stones and gems found on the islands.

Wildlife in New Zealand

New Zealand has a huge variety of animals and birds, many unique to the country, including the world's largest parrot, the kakapo.

1. KOTUKU (WHITE HERON)
2. KAKAPO
3. KIWI
4. FJORDLAND SKINK
5. FUR SEAL

The Canterbury Plains

The Southern Alps rise high above the fertile Canterbury Plains on South Island. These plains, though small in area, are New Zealand's most important farming region. Here sheep are grazed and wheat, barley, and potatoes are produced. New Zealand is the world's leading exporter of lamb and mutton.

The All Blacks

Many New Zealanders are enthusiastic supporters of rugby football. The All Blacks, so called because of the color of their uniform, are the national team. Before play starts the All Blacks perform a traditional Maori dance.

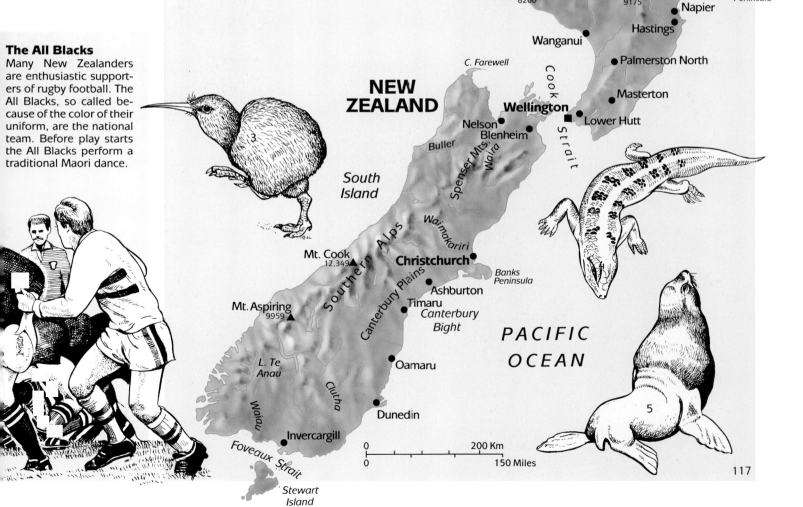

North Cape

Whangarei

Great Barrier Island

Takapuna

Auckland　Manukau

Bay of Plenty

Tauranga

East Cape

Hamilton

North Island

Waipa

Waikato

Whakatane

Rotorua

Gisborne

New Plymouth

Wanganui

L. Taupo

Mahia Peninsula

Mt. Egmont 8260

▲ Ruapehu 9175

Napier

Wanganui

Hastings

C. Farewell

Palmerston North

NEW ZEALAND

Cook Strait

Masterton

Wellington　Lower Hutt

Nelson

Blenheim

Buller

Spenser Mts.

Waira

South Island

Waimakariri

Southern Alps

Mt. Cook 12,349 ▲

Christchurch

Banks Peninsula

Mt. Aspiring 9959 ▲

Canterbury Plains

Ashburton

Timaru

Canterbury Bight

L. Te Anau

PACIFIC OCEAN

Clutha

Oamaru

Waiau

Dunedin

Foveaux Strait

Invercargill

| 0 | | 200 Km |
| 0 | | 150 Miles |

Stewart Island

117

PACIFIC ISLANDS

The islands scattered across the Pacific Ocean, southeast of Asia, are grouped into three regions: Melanesia (which includes Papua New Guinea), Micronesia, and Polynesia which extends north to Hawaii and east to include Easter Island.

The original settlers of the islands are thought to have come by sea from southeast Asia. Today the Pacific islanders are still expert seafarers, and many of the smaller islands' economies rely on fishing. Much of the agriculture on the islands is subsistence farming. In the tropical climate yams, breadfruit, sweet potatoes, and fruits are grown and sold in local markets. Larger islands such as Papua New Guinea also grow coffee, copra, and cocoa for export. Valuable mineral reserves on some islands are an important source of income: New Caledonia is the third largest producer of nickel in the world, Christmas Island has large phosphate supplies, and copper is mined on Papua New Guinea.

South Sea paradise
This idyllic view near Bora Bora in the French Polynesian islands is typical of much of the scenery in the South Seas. The beauty of the surroundings and the tropical climate are attracting more and more visitors every year. Some islands are developing luxury resorts to encourage the extra revenue that tourism brings.

Map of Fiji

```
0          150 Km
0        100 Miles
FIJI
```

Vanua Levu — Udu Pt. — Ringgold Is.
Lambasa — Rambi
Yasawa Group — Bligh Water — Taveuni — Nanuku Passage
Viti Levu — Koro — Vanua Mbalavu — Lau (Eastern) Group
Lautoka — Tavua — Mango
▲Tomanlivi 1322 — Ovalau — KORO SEA — Thithia
Singatoka — Ngau — Lakemba Passage
Suva — Lakemba
Vatulele — Kandavu Passage — Moala
Totoya — Kambara
Kandavu — Matuku

Modern ways
Until recently, many of the Pacific islands were undeveloped and the people lived as they had for thousands of years. Development of the islands by outsiders has changed the traditional way of life dramatically. Younger people in particular have adopted many "western" ways.

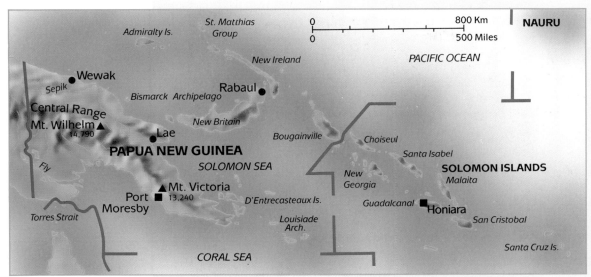

St. Matthias Group
Admiralty Is.
NAURU
PACIFIC OCEAN
New Ireland
Wewak
Sepik
Rabaul
Bismarck Archipelago
New Britain
Central Range
Mt. Wilhelm ▲
14,790
Lae
Bougainville
Choiseul
Santa Isabel
SOLOMON ISLANDS
PAPUA NEW GUINEA
SOLOMON SEA
Malaita
New Georgia
Fly
Mt. Victoria
Port ■ 13,240
Moresby
D'Entrecasteaux Is.
Guadalcanal ■ Honiara
San Cristobal
Torres Strait
Louisiade Arch.
Santa Cruz Is.
CORAL SEA

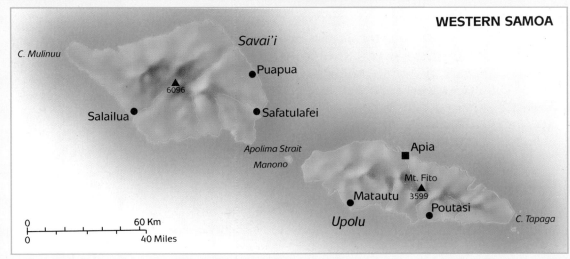

WESTERN SAMOA
Savai'i
C. Mulinuu
Puapua
▲ 6096
Safatulafei
Salailua
Apolima Strait
Apia ■
Manono
Mt. Fito
▲ 3599
Matautu
Poutasi
Upolu
C. Tapaga
0 — 60 Km
0 — 40 Miles

Coconut wealth

Copra, the dry white flesh of the coconut, being stored at Port Moresby Wharf in Papua New Guinea, ready for export. Copra brings wealth to many Pacific islands. It is prepared by removing the fibrous husk of the coconut, splitting the nut and laying out strips of the white "meat" to dry in the sun. The meat is then crushed to extract the oil.

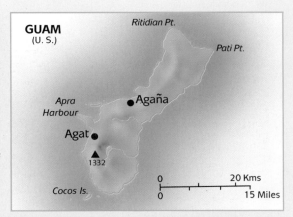

GUAM
(U. S.)
Ritidian Pt.
Pati Pt.
Apra Harbour
Agaña
Agat
▲ 1332
Cocos Is.
0 — 20 Kms
0 — 15 Miles

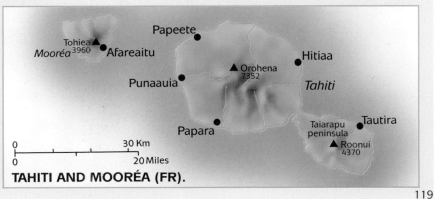

Papeete
Tohiea ▲
Mooréa 3960 ● Afareaitu
Hitiaa
▲ Orohena
7352
Tahiti
Punaauia
Papara
Taiarapu peninsula
▲ Roonui
4370
Tautira
0 — 30 Km
0 — 20 Miles
TAHITI AND MOORÉA (FR).

ARCTIC AND ANTARCTICA

The Arctic and Antarctica are remote, icebound regions around the two Poles. At the North Pole a layer of ice about 20 feet deep floats within the Arctic Ocean. At the South Pole the ice cap is on average 7500 feet thick over the buried landmass of Antarctica.

Both regions are extremely cold. However, during summer in the northern hemisphere the snow and ice melt in parts of the Arctic, and moss, lichen, and flowers appear. About two million people live within the Arctic Circle, including the Inuit of Alaska and Greenland. No one lives permanently in Antarctica, although scientists have set up camps there to study the environment.

The Arctic is rich in mineral resources including fossil fuels, diamonds and gold. These are being exploited by the surrounding countries. Antarctica is rich in food resources from the sea, but in accordance with international agreement, it has remained untouched so far.

Research in Antarctica

Explorers first reached Antarctica in the early part of this century. Today, researchers from many countries have set up stations in the inhospitable conditions, even growing their own vegetables in heated greenhouses. Nineteen nations

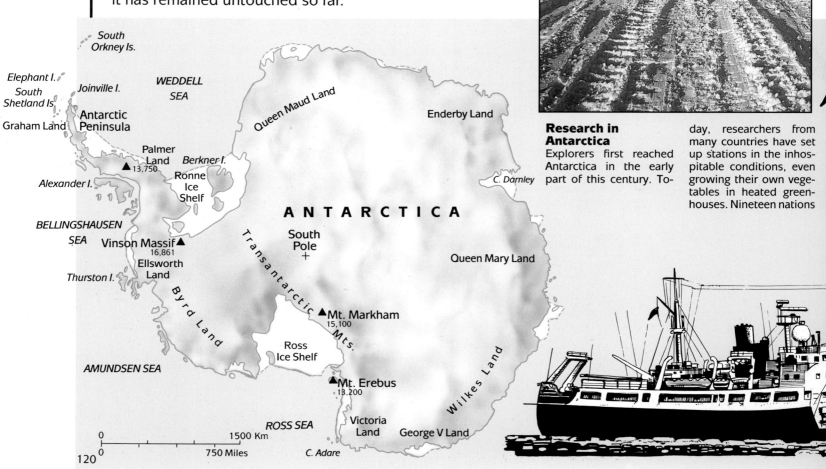

South Orkney Is.
Elephant I.
South Shetland Is.
Joinville I.
WEDDELL SEA
Queen Maud Land
Enderby Land
Antarctic Peninsula
Graham Land
Palmer Land
▲13,750
Berkner I.
Ronne Ice Shelf
Alexander I.
C. Darnley
BELLINGSHAUSEN SEA
ANTARCTICA
South Pole +
Vinson Massif ▲
16,861
Ellsworth Land
Thurston I.
Queen Mary Land
Byrd Land
Transantarctic Mts.
▲ Mt. Markham
15,100
AMUNDSEN SEA
Ross Ice Shelf
▲ Mt. Erebus
13,200
Wilkes Land
ROSS SEA
Victoria Land
George V Land
C. Adare

0 — 1500 Km
0 — 750 Miles

Animals in the cold

The Poles and the surrounding seas support a huge variety of wildlife, despite the extreme cold.
1. ARCTIC SKUA
2. POLAR BEAR
3. WALRUS
4. KILLER WHALE

have laid claim to the potential wealth buried in Antarctica, and many more are interested. In a treaty signed in 1961, the 19 nations agreed to conserve the region.

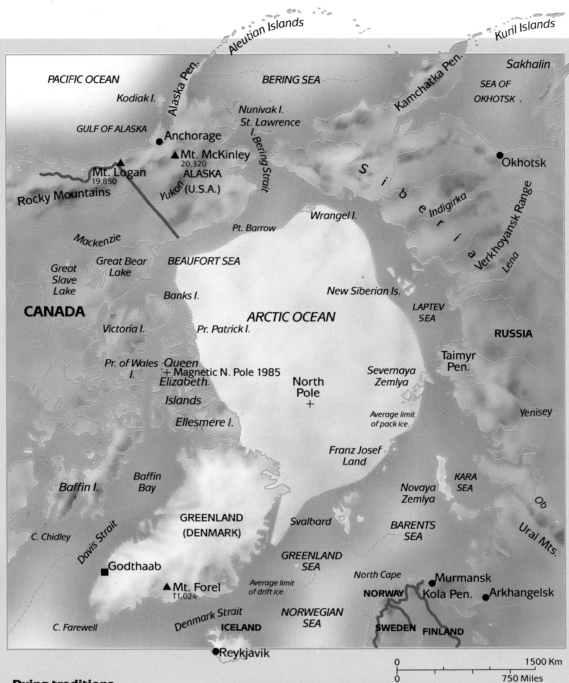

PACIFIC OCEAN

Kodiak I.

GULF OF ALASKA

Anchorage

▲ Mt. McKinley
20,320

Mt. Logan
19,850

ALASKA

Rocky Mountains

Yukon (U.S.A.)

Mackenzie

Great Bear Lake

Great Slave Lake

Banks I.

CANADA

Victoria I.

Pr. Patrick I.

Pr. of Wales I.

Queen
+ Magnetic N. Pole 1985
Elizabeth
Islands

Ellesmere I.

Baffin I.

Baffin Bay

C. Chidley

Davis Strait

GREENLAND
(DENMARK)

Godthaab

▲ Mt. Forel
11,024

C. Farewell

Denmark Strait

ICELAND

Reykjavik

Aleutian Islands

Kuril Islands

BERING SEA

Kamchatka Pen.

Sakhalin

SEA OF OKHOTSK

Nunivak I.
St. Lawrence I.

Bering Strait

Okhotsk

Siberia

Indigirka

Verkhoyansk Range

Lena

Wrangel I.

Pt. Barrow

BEAUFORT SEA

New Siberian Is.

ARCTIC OCEAN

LAPTEV SEA

RUSSIA

Taimyr Pen.

North Pole
+

Severnaya Zemlya

Yenisey

Average limit of pack ice.

Franz Josef Land

KARA SEA

Novaya Zemlya

Ob

Ural Mts.

Svalbard

BARENTS SEA

GREENLAND SEA

North Cape

Murmansk

NORWAY

Kola Pen.

Arkhangelsk

Average limit of drift ice.

NORWEGIAN SEA

SWEDEN

FINLAND

0 — 1500 Km
0 — 750 Miles

Dying traditions

The ancestors of these Inuit children lived in isolated communities in the Arctic, and survived by hunting and fishing. They caught caribou and reindeer, which provided them with meat, and skins for making clothes and tents. When they moved on to search for food, teams of dogs pulled the sleds.

Today the Arctic is no longer so isolated. Since the discovery of oil, mining communities have sprung up and with them schools, shops, and hospitals. The traditional way of life has been destroyed and most of the Inuit now live in permanent homes in these mining communities.

121

GENERAL INDEX

Page numbers in *italics* refer to illustrations

MAP INDEX

Page numbers in **bold** refer to entries in information files

125

Acknowledgments
The publishers would like to thank the following for the use of their pictures:

ZEFA Picture Library is indicated as **Z** throughout
Tony Stone Worldwide is indicated as **TSW** throughout
Robert Harding Picture Library is indicated as **RHPL** throughout

Page 1 TSW/S. & N. Geary; p3 TSW; p24 TSW/J. Kopee; p26 *middle* Z/Hunter *bottom* Z/K. Kummels; p27 TSW; p28 *middle* RHPL *bottom* Z; p29 RHPL; p30 Z; p31 RHPL/Howard Greaves; p32 TSW/D. Schultz; p33 TSW; p34 *top* TSW/M. Segal *middle* Z/Stefnmans *bottom* RHPL/G. & P. Lorrigan; p35 TSW/M. Brooke; p36 Z; p37 TSW/Lev Nisnevich; p38 *left* Holt Studios *right* Z; p39 TSW/Robert Frerck; p40 *left* Z *right* RHPL; p41 TSW/Ed Pritchard; p42 *left* Z *right* TSW/Charles Thatcher; p43 RHPL; p44 Z, p45 *left* TSW/G. Prentice *right* RHPL/G. & P. Lorrigan; p46 Hutchison Library/P. Wolmuth; p46 *top* RHPL *bottom* TSW/W. Rudolph; p48 TSW/P. Gittoes; p49 Z; p50 TSW; p51 Z; p52 *left* Art Directors *top right* TSW/S. Cunningham *bottom right* Z/J. Heydecker; p54 *left* TSW/D. Levy *right* Hutchison Library; p55 *top* TSW/D. Levy *bottom* TSW/T. Zimmerman; p56 TSW/R. Passmore; p58 *top* Z/Eugen *middle* Z/Strachil; p59 TSW/N. Beer; p60 *top right* Z/Damm *bottom left* Z/Edel *bottom right* Danish Dairy Board; p61 Z/Eugen; p62 *left* TSW/D. Higgs *right* TSW; p63 TSW; p64 *left* RHPL/R. Curdy *right* TSW/C. Kempf; p65 *top* French Railways *middle* Magnum/Zachmann; p66 *left* Z/Streichen *right* TSW/J. Yates; p67 Netherlands Board of Tourism; p68 *left* TSW/R. Everts *right* Z/Deuter; p69 Carla Arnold/Praktica; p70 *left* Z/R. Nicholas *right* TSW/M. Mehlig; p71 TSW; p72 *left* Fiat *right* Hutchison Picture Library; p73 TSW/M. Mehlig; p74 *left* TSW/S. Johnson *right* TSW/O. Benn; p75 Magnum/M. Gruyaert; p76 *left* TSW/R. Everts *right* TSW/M. Caldwell; p77 *top* Z/Dr. H. Kramarz *bottom* Z; p78 *left* TSW/R. Everts *right* Z; p79 Magnum/E. Erwitt; p80 Frank Spooner Pictures/V. Shone; p81 Z; p82 *top* Linda Proud *middle* Z *bottom* Novosti; p83 Z; p84 TSW; p86 *top* Z/Maroon *middle* Z; p88 *left* Mepha/Jill Brown *right* Sonia Halliday; p89 *top* Z *bottom* TSW; p90 *left* Planet Earth/ H.C. Heaps *right* Z; p91 TSW; p92 *left* RHPL *right* Z/K. Schulz; p93 *top* TSW *middle* RHPL; p94 *left* TSW/A. Smith *right* Z/H. Raze; p95 Z/Sunak; p96 RHPL; p97 TSW; p98 *middle* TSW/A. le Garsmeur *bottom* TSW/Osmond; p99 Hutchison Picture Library; p100 *top* TSW *middle, bottom* TSW/A. le Garsmeur; p101 TSW/Ed Pritchard; p102 *left* TSW/McCooey *right* TSW; p103 *top* Hutchison Picture Library *bottom* TSW; p104 Frank Spooner Pictures; p106 Z; p107 Frank Spooner Pictures/M. Deville; p108 *left* Hutchison Picture Library *right* Z/E. Earp; p109 TSW; p110 *left* TSW/I. Murphy *right* RHPL/C. Jopp; p111 Hutchison Picture Library; p114 *left* TSW/S. & N. Geary *right* TSW; p115 TSW; p116 TSW/R. Smith; p117 TSW; p118 Z/E. Christian; p119 RHPL; p120 RHPL/G. Renner; p121 RHPL/W. Herbert.

Picture Research by Linda Proud